The
Disciplined
Life-style

The Disciplined Life-style

Richard S. Taylor

 Bethany Fellowship INC.
MINNEAPOLIS, MINNESOTA 55438

This printing, 1981

Quotations from *The Berkeley Version in Modern English* (copyright © 1945, 1958, 1959 by Zondervan Publishing House) used by permission.
Quotations from *The New Testament in Modern English* (copyright © 1958 by J. B. Phillips) used by permission of The Macmillan Company.

Published in 1973 and 1975 under the title: *A Return to Christian Culture*

The Disciplined Life-style
Richard S. Taylor

Library of Congress Catalog Card Number 80-65581

ISBN 0-87123-110-7

Published by Bethany Fellowship, Inc.
6820 Auto Club Road, Minneapolis, Minnesota 55438

Printed in the United States of America

Dedication

To my esteemed friends
C. H. Ripper, Ph.D.
Administrative Vice-president
and
Mel-Thomas Rothwell, Ph.D.
Professor of Philosophy
whose kindness in inviting me to deliver the
Ripper-Rothwell Lectures at Bethany Nazarene College
in February, 1972, compelled me to hammer into
some sort of reasonable form these convictions
which have gripped my thinking for some years.

About the Author

Richard S. Taylor, MA., Th.D., graduated from Cascade College, Portland, Oregon, and Pasadena College, Pasadena, California, and took his Th.D. degree at Boston University. He served on the faculty of the Nazarene Theological Seminary in Kansas City for 16 years as a professor of theology and missions, until his retirement in 1977. He is now Professor Emeritus of Theology and Missions.

Acknowledgments

Appreciation is expressed to the following for permission to use copyrighted materials as indicated:

Inter-Varsity Press, Downers Grove, Ill., for quotations from *Modern Art and the Death of a Culture*, by H. R. Rookmaaker, copyright 1970.

Zondervan Publishing House, Grand Rapids, Mich., for a quotation from *Get Your Hands off my Throat*, by David Wilkerson, copyright 1971.

Foreword

A new book by Richard S. Taylor is always an event. Since his first work, *The Right Conception of Sin* (written when he was 27), Dr. Taylor has exerted an increasing influence among evangelicals in general and Wesleyans in particular.

This book on the theology of culture is both Christian and contemporary, addressing the perennial problem of Christ and culture. As the end-time community of the Spirit, the Church is the herald and harbinger of God's coming kingdom. As such it derives its life and holiness from the risen Lord, who is yet to transform the kingdoms of this world into the kingdom of God. But it carries out its mission in sinful human society. As God's new creation, the Church represents the age to come, but in its historical form it lives and works in the present evil age.

This volume is a discerning application of Rom. 12:2: "Don't let the world around you squeeze you into its own mold, but let God remold your minds from within" (J. B. Phillips). Richard Taylor, who always "sees life steadily and sees it whole," reveals both deep Christian understanding and a wide knowledge of the social milieu in which the Church of the seventies finds itself. He makes a penetrating Christian analysis of our "plastic society" as well as the "counter culture" of those who have repudiated the "establishment." And as he does so he gives a *prescription* for a Christian approach to culture.

Dr. Taylor makes a plea for *Christian* culture. He believes that Christ came to remold our *total* lives—not only our spirits, but also our intellects; not only our moral existence, but also our aesthetics. And this not simply to the end that we become merely cultured, but that we may be able to discharge the responsibilities of Christian stewardship to our society and the world. He has written, "not to encourage a cultural approach to religion, but a religious approach to culture."

—WILLIAM M. GREATHOUSE
President, Nazarene Theological Seminary

Preface

This book is written in the conviction that as Christians we have suffered immeasurable loss because we have almost ignored the matter of culture. We have failed to see it as a large and significant factor in personal spiritual growth and have been only half awake to its extremely important role in evangelism.

In addition, we have shared with our contemporaries an insufficient awareness of the part culture plays in many current social tensions. It is very likely, for instance, that the race problem is more a matter of culture than of color. The "generation gap," also, is not so much chronological as cultural. And most certainly culture is a huge factor in the persistence of poverty.

As far as the Church is concerned, the problem of difficult congregations could be in many cases more a matter of culture than of carnality. Highly cultured people are more apt to temper their strong notions with understanding and fair play. They are more appreciative and less crotchety. Other things being equal, the lower the culture, the greater the pettiness and obstinacy. (But by no means should culture be confused with wealth.)

And the shoe fits the pastoral foot too. Why do preachers fail? Some never in a whole lifetime of valiant effort quite measure up to their potential, and come to the end with a deep hurt and bewilderment. We might be astonished if we knew how many times this almost-made-it kind of failure could be traced, not to a spiritual lack, or to indolence or insincerity, but to glaring cultural defects.

If culture is so important, is it not time that we attempted to do some serious thinking about it? The purpose of this little volume is to introduce some of the issues which are directly related to Christian growth on the one hand, and Christian stewardship on the other. Perhaps together we can begin to give this vital dimension of Christian life and service the serious attention it warrants. For too long culture has been the Cinderella of the household.

At the heart of this book is an examination of the relation of culture to the holy life. Many suppose there is no organic relation at all; that holiness has nothing authoritative to say about culture; and that, while holiness is essential, culture is inconsequential. The author sincerely hopes that these discussions will disabuse our minds completely and permanently of this fiction.

The strong conviction expressed so far demands that the question no longer be deferred: What is culture? While the answer will be developed in different ways throughout the following chapters, a brief preliminary statement is necessary. The term has a technical meaning as used by the scientific anthropologist. In this sense culture "is the work of men's minds and hands," writes H. Richard Niebuhr.[1] It is what men have done with the raw material of their earthly setting. As nature is the gift of God, culture is the work of man. As such, the culture of a society may be primitive or advanced and highly technological. In either case, the term includes the totality of the life pattern—language, religion, literature (if any), machines and inventions, arts and crafts, architecture and decor, dress, laws, customs, marriage and family structures, government and institutions, plus the peculiar and characteristic ways of thinking and acting.

Obviously in this broad sense everyone is *in* a culture. It may be Western or Eastern, American or Japanese, or whatever. There are many ways cultures can be divided and classified. And often within a general culture are various subcultures, perhaps even *counter* cultures, such as "hippieism" or "Afroism."

But the term "culture" also has a specialized and quite personal meaning, more particularly relevant to the individual. On this level everyone not only is *in* a culture but *has* a culture. This is the life-style and accomplishments which he has acquired. It may be typical of the culture of his environment; if so, he will have no problem in identifying and relating. Or it may be atypical, and as such disjoined and disoriented. To the extent that one's personal culture is irregular will one have difficulty in relating comfortably to his immediate social environment.

At this point we must introduce two new adjectives: poor and good. While everyone has a culture it may be poor by the standards of one's contemporaries. In this case they are apt to see him as crude and inept, a misfit, and perhaps give him a wide berth. He does not represent them well. He is an enigma to them—probably an embarrassment.

It is only when a person has gone to the trouble of acquiring the traits and life-styles most acceptable to his society that he can be said to be *cultured*. Thus, when "culture" is turned into an adjective it means *highly developed*. One of Webster's definitions includes *tastes*: "enlightenment and excellence of taste acquired by intellectual and aesthetic training." The word "acquired" reminds us of Niebuhr's distinction: "The gifts of nature are received as they are communicated without any human intent or conscious effort; but the gifts of culture cannot be possessed without striving on the part of the recipient."[2]

It becomes clear then that any discussion of culture must always keep in mind two levels, societal and personal. Similarly there are two kinds of approach—the *descriptive* and the *prescriptive*. The anthropologist merely describes a culture as he finds it; he does not prescribe what it ought to be. But the Christian must prescribe, like it or not, for he cannot be content with poor culture, and he refuses to accept the premise that one culture is as good as another (whether in a society or in an individual). He is a "Christian horticulturist" in the garden of the human soul.

One day while in Japan, we watched some gardeners working on small roadside pine trees. Upon inquiry we were told, "They are trimming them so as to improve their personalities." If trees need better "personalities," people do too! Therefore the Christian had better go to work, if not on others, at least on himself. There may be a lot of trimming to do.

—RICHARD S. TAYLOR

Contents

1

A Christian Approach to Culture

"Character—Culture—Christ." This college motto* provides a perfect "pad" for the launching of these studies. The three *C*'s help at the outset to make two things clear.

First, in this book the term "culture" will be used *primarily* in the way the college motto uses it; that is, with a restricted, specialized meaning. It is distinct from character, which is what we are in heart. We may have good character but bad culture. The reverse is also true: a highly cultured man may be a scoundrel. Culture is also different from religion. One may be a Christian, even an intensely devout follower of Christ, yet be uncultured; or—by the same token —one may be a cultured infidel.

*Bethany Nazarene College, Bethany, Okla.

What then is this specialized sense which we have in mind? *Culture is the development of the person, intellectually, aesthetically, and socially, to the full use of his powers, in compatibility with the recognized standards of excellence of his society.*

The second thing the college motto suggests is the relation of Christ to culture. This relationship has two aspects. One, Christ is related to culture exactly as He is related to character. When Christ is the Molder of character we have Christian character; precisely, when Christ is the molder of culture we have Christian culture. This is crucial, for it needs to be stated at the outset that our goal is not just conventional culture but *Christian* culture. Christian culture is shaped by Christ.

A Christian Obligation

The other facet of Christ's relationship to culture is a little more subtle. Perhaps it can be stated this way. Christ is the Tie that binds character and culture together in mutual obligation. They may remain distinct, but cease to be independent. They make demands on each other for the simple reason that both character and culture are aspects of our stewardship in Christ. Good stewardship requires good character; this we all know. But it requires good culture as well; this we have too often forgotten. For not only is our character a credit or discredit to our Lord, but our culture is as well. Therefore total stewardship forbids the fragmentation of our development. We cannot be faithful to Christ by saying, "I'll cultivate my spiritual life exclusively, and disregard self-improvement along other lines." As Harry Blamires puts it: "There is no room in Christendom for a culture of the spirit which neglects the mind, for a discipline of the will which by-passes the intellect."[1]

When Christ is discerned clearly, we see that He is the Keystone which binds character and culture into one strong, symmetrical arch of Christian personality. We must affirm then that at the deepest level there can be no *mature* Christian character which despises culture, any more than there can be a truly Christian culture which is not rooted in character. But it is in Christ that this indestructible synthesis is found.

The aforementioned motto therefore has led us straight to the first proposition in defining a Christian approach to culture, namely, that as "cleanliness is next to godliness," so *culture is next to character as a handmaiden in Christian stewardship.* While not equal as far as salvation is concerned (for it is holiness, not polish, "without which no man shall see the Lord"), it is not too far behind character as an essential qualification for Christian service. Love for Christ therefore will see in the task of becoming cultured the urgency of an imperative.

Let us pause here a little longer. Being saved and being civil are admittedly not the same. But it is time we were getting the two together. Not only are we engulfed in a tide of barbarism around us, but some misguided Christians seem to think it is pious to be uncultured. It is not. Just as a civilized man should also be a Christian, so should a Christian also be civilized. And no man is civilized who is not civil. Nor is any man educated who is not cultured. We should have in one person a fusion of zeal and tact, courage and courtesy, holiness and orderliness, godliness and cleanliness, convictions and intelligence, piety and good taste. The Christian who is inwardly sincere but outwardly cheap has created for his Christian witness a huge and needless credibility gap.

Becoming personally cultured is therefore a Christian obligation.

Prescriptive, Not Descriptive

The second proposition is simple to state, but not so simple to clarify. It is this: *A Christian approach to culture is prescriptive, not merely descriptive.* While this idea was anticipated in the preface, it now needs to be expanded.

Within a given culture (as seen by the anthropologist), a cultured person (in the sense we have established) would be one who would be acknowledged by that culture as most typically representing it. He would be one who honored its language by properly using it; one who was acquainted with the customs and courtesies and who practiced them; one who was expert in at least some of its arts and crafts; and one who in his thinking, feelings, and personal life-style was representative of the acknowledged best in his society. Naturally, therefore, we would expect to find many differences between a cultured Japanese and a cultured American, a cultured Arab and a cultured Argentinian. Even if all these "cultures" were Christianized, differences would still exist.

The fact that a man is deemed cultured or uncultured in terms of the ethnic and societal culture of which he is a part proves that, even though an outsider studying that culture might aim simply at *describing* it, the culture itself has *prescriptive* disciplines for all who participate in it. That is, there are those who dictate (prescribe) what a person must learn and become if he is to be accepted as cultured. This is as true in New Guinea (on a primitive level) as it is in Norway, as true among Eskimos as among Mexicans. In a country such as the United States, with over 200 million people comprising many cross-cultures and subcultures, it might be difficult to secure a consensus. But the diversity would be in external detail, not so much in principle.

To be more specific: It is likely that all would agree that to be recognized as cultured within any homogeneous social or ethnic unit, a person would be marked by at least six characteristics:

1. *A cultivated mind.* This is the intellectual dimension.
2. *Cultivated speech and voice.* This is the communicative dimension.

3. *Cultivated manners.* This is the interpersonal dimension.

4. *A cultivated social sense.* This is the community dimension.

5. *Cultivated tastes.* This is the aesthetic dimension.

6. *Cultivated abilities and skills.* This is the vocational dimension.

Let us run through these again. In any general culture, a man will not be considered cultured by his contemporaries who is mentally lazy, dull, and uninformed. "The spirit of learning is integral to the highest and noblest impulses of human nature," writes Fred P. Thompson, Jr.[2]

Also, his culture will be rated as defective if he has no facility in the use of his mother tongue, sufficient to articulate his thoughts with reasonable correctness and clarity, and do it with a pleasing, well-modulated voice. The importance of the voice is underscored by Dr. Horace G. Ranskopt, professor of speech at the University of Washington, who says, "People judge us almost as quickly by our voices as they do by our appearance." He further claims that "mellow tones pleasant to the ear" indicate emotional balance.[3]

Furthermore, a person will not be classed as cultured if he is impolite, crude, and offensive. The Roman "philosopher king," Marcus Aurelius, said: "There is a proper dignity and proportion to be observed in the performance of every act of life." A similar sentiment was expressed by Edward George Bulwer-Lytton, the nineteenth-century English novelist. He observed that cultured people are marked by a disciplined quietness in all they do. "They eat in quiet, move in quiet, live in quiet, and lose even their money in quiet; while low persons cannot take up either a spoon or an affront without making an amazing noise about it."

Nor will one be thought cultured if he is not socialized. If he sees no personal obligation to society; if he is blind to the importance of that cohesion in society which depends upon respect for its laws and customs; if he is insensitive to people around him, utterly disregarding their needs, feelings, and rights, he can hardly be called cultured. (This is what brands most tobacco users as defective in culture; few of them have the slightest concern for the health, comfort, feelings, or rights of nonsmokers.)

The same negative judgment will prevail if a person obviously shows poor taste in dress, diction, arts, and artifacts.

Neither will one be considered cultured if he has not disciplined himself in the achievement of some kind of mastery—some skill or knowledge—which makes him a producer rather than merely a consumer, and assures him the vocational respect of his fellows. For certainly a leech who bleeds parents and social agencies as a voluntary way of life, who is an economic hitchhiker, who rides through life piggyback, has no valid claim to being thought cultured, no matter how soft his accents or gentle his manner.

These are the canons of culture on which, I suspect, there would be basic agreement anywhere in the world. The details (as has already been noted) would vary infinitely. Standards of good manners would be different in China from what they are in America, Canada, or Britain. When a Chinese has enjoyed his dinner and wishes to show his appreciation, it is polite to belch loudly; in Western countries the hostess would be quite shocked. But the underlying principle is the same: There *is* a recognized etiquette and no person is considered cultured who does not know it and observe it.

As a passing observation at this point, it may be noted that one of the surest proofs of the possession—or lack—of this high degree of personal culture is the leisure test. The person who really meets the six requirements will have cultural resources for the wise use of private time. You will never find a truly cultured person bored because he has nothing to do. He will have so many interests, his mind will be so alert and curious, he will have so many exciting projects up his sleeve, that when cast on his own resources, with time on his hands, he will not be at a loss for some creative and useful activity. He can adapt himself either to people or to solitude. No one needs to entertain him. This is why habitual TV gawking is not only a low level of cultural activity, but often the sign of a poverty-stricken mind. It takes no *T.V* initiative, no creativity, no imagination, no effort to watch a TV program. The willingness to spend hour upon hour this way simply advertises a basic cultural emptiness—the bottom of the idea barrel has been scraped. As far as Christians are concerned, there is shame in the comment: "Many people who yearn for immortality don't know what to do on a rainy Sunday afternoon." For boredom is a sickness of the small mind, not the product of dull circumstances.

Now let us return to our main line of thought. The six canons of general culture listed above imply a *prescriptive* approach to culture. While no modern society would claim absolute perfection for its culture, it nevertheless has standards of excellence toward which it seeks to educate its people. If a cultured man is marked by cultivated speech, then there must be basic standards by which his speech can be judged. Even though these standards are constantly undergoing change and are frequently the subject of debate, they are nevertheless there, and they are sufficiently established and diffused throughout society that the average educated audience can tell in five minutes whether the speaker is literate or illiterate.

In the broad sense, educational institutions are necessarily prescriptive in their approach to culture, as is witnessed by every curriculum designed to lead a student toward clearly defined goals and levels of attainment. Particularly is this seen in the fine arts, the bellwether of culture. That the fine arts is prescriptive is confessed by every serious and responsible school of music, painting, or sculpture in the world. A school isn't in the business of telling beginners that their work is as good as the master's, but of showing them how they can also achieve a measure of excellence. This is avowedly and unapologetically a judgmental stance. Even if everything is called art, Joanne Bryers insists that "it is necessary to decide that one work and not another has authority; and this one and not that one expands senses and compels the imagination."[4]

Implicit in teaching is the assumption that the good is different from the poor, and that there are standards of excellence by which the good can be discerned. There is the further assumption that the poor ought to become good, and the good ought to become better, and that at the top are experts who can tell along what lines improvement needs to be made. Over 30 years ago, J. Gresham Machen, of Princeton fame, said: "Until the artistic impulse is eradicated more thoroughly from human life than has so far been done, even by the best efforts of the metallic civilization of our day, we cannot get rid of the categories of good and bad or high and low in the field of art."[5]

A Christianized Culture

As has been stated, Christianity is *prescriptive* in its approach to culture. We must reiterate that Christ is not indifferent to our culture. He cares about what we are as total persons. He enlists in His service character *and* culture; heart, head, and hand. As Francis Schaeffer says, "God is interested in the whole man and also in the culture which flows from men's relationships with each other."[6]

Christianity prescribes the culture we should acquire, if we are to best glorify Christ. It prescribes in three ways:

First, *it endorses the basic canons of culture.* We cannot serve our society unless in some sense we are identified with it. It is a Christian obligation to become cultured according to the best standards of one's society, if one would carry the greatest weight with that society in representing Christ. Jesus was a typical Jew of His day, in respect to

22

their best traits and qualities. It is unthinkable that He should be smelly or unkempt by Jewish standards, or that He should deliberately trample underfoot the customary amenities and social customs. At times He violated the religious codes, such as failing to wash ceremonially before eating, but every such breach was for the purpose of teaching a lesson. His disciples were admittedly a motley crowd—some of them, perhaps, even a bit crude when they were first called. But Jesus refined them, as is seen by His pointed instructions concerning their behavior when He sent them out two by two (Luke 10:3-8). In the post-Pentecost era, all of the apostles, especially Paul, the trained scholar and Hebrew gentleman, could move about the Roman and Hellenistic world with ease and grace, and commanded respect everywhere they went. And Paul certainly demanded a high level of acceptable culture in his preachers (I Tim. 3:1-7; Titus 1:5-9)!

As for the intellectual aspect of culture, Fred P. Thompson observes that language "as the vehicle of thought and the conservator of truth has always been regarded as a priceless treasure by the molders of Christian tradition." Therefore, he argues that "the enterprise of learning . . . [is a] Christian imperative." He concludes: "Since we are Christian men, we are under mandate to acquire such competence and skill in handling the Word of Truth as to merit the approval of its ultimate Author. Only the learned man can be a whole man, a cultivated man, a mature man, and thus in the finest sense, a Christian man."[7]

Second, *Christianity impregnates culture with its own principles.* In this way it becomes Christian culture. Christianity *purifies* culture by purifying its ethics. Then, Christianity *humanizes* culture by infusing it with Christian love. This kind of love is the real secret of courtliness and good manners. He who loves is at ease with others, and they are at ease with him. Christian love prompts the best in courtesy, not as an affectation, but out of true regard for the other per-

23

son. Christian love prompts that kind of dress and deportment which expresses respect for ourselves, our neighbors, and our Christ. Christian love directs all the attainments of the cultured mind, the clever tongue, and the skilled hand—not along lines of insincere self-serving, which smiles to get attention or flatters to get its way, but along lines of genuine goodwill and what someone has called "proximate compassion." Many would-be cultured people are compassionate in the abstract—idealistically and romantically—but always at a distance. The immediate heartbreak, the immediate anguish, the situation at hand which calls for compassion, perhaps even in their own home, they don't even see. Yet this is the plus factor in culture which makes it Christian, and as such, a beautiful thing.

It would be of inestimable profit to observe how many of the admonitions in the Epistles are as closely related to culture as to ethics. Here are two samples from Colossians: "Clothe yourselves with tenderness of heart, kindliness, humble-mindedness, gentleness, patient endurance"; and this one—"Conduct yourselves wisely toward the outsiders, using your time to the best possible advantage. Let your speech always be gracious and so well reasoned out that you will know how to reply to each individual" (Col. 3:12; 4:5-6, Berkeley).

Third, *Christianity challenges and rejects that in any general culture which is evil and irredeemable.* We have assumed to this point that much in any culture is spiritually and morally neutral. It can be either Christianized or paganized. It does not need to be westernized to be devoted to the service of Christ.

Only in recent years have Christian missionaries begun to learn this. Christianizing a nation does not mean Americanizing or Anglicizing it. Far too many missionaries have failed the culture test. They either could not distinguish between that which was innocent and that which was inherently evil (and thus created unnecessary and artificial obstacles)

24

or they have not sufficiently adapted themselves to the innocent features of the host culture. In a certain country, good manners demand that when the hostess offers you more food you say no, until she has asked you the third time. One missionary snorted, "That's silly. If my guests want more, let them say yes when I offer it. They needn't think I'm going to offer it three times just to toady to their custom." She didn't last long.

But having said all of that, we must face the raw fact that in any culture shaped by centuries of paganism will be found many things which cannot be sanctified. In some respects Paul made himself "all things to all men," but not when sexual immorality or idolatry or social oppression were concerned. The Christian Church challenged non-Christian customs and standards head on. When it came to monogamy versus polygamy, family relationships, sexual promiscuity, business dishonesty or class snobbishness, and personal habits of industry, sobriety, and orderliness, the New Testament makes no allowance for a gradual reeducation or a step-by-step adjustment. It is all the way right now. A Christian standard is raised, and converts (as seen for instance in Paul's letters to the young church at Thessalonica) are told, This is the way you must live. Much of this is primarily ethical, no doubt; but always ethics affects culture, since the two are in constant interaction. A practice is clearly not assimilable by the Church just because it is a custom of long standing and general acceptance.

It is to be expected therefore that where the gospel goes there will be not only radical ethical changes but cultural changes as well. Many such will involve painful dislocations within the society affected. But even though painful they are much needed healing correctives. For instance, the news media reported in 1971 that thousands of Bangladesh women who were raped by the Pakistani soldiers and who as a result became pregnant were socially ostracized, banished from jobs, from their husbands (or parents) and homes. This is a custom which is a part of the national culture. But it is an inhuman, monstrous culture that would condemn innocent women and their unfortunate children to such a merciless, tragic doom. If Bangladesh should become Christianized, its culture at that point would be changed.

Perhaps H. R. Rookmaaker, professor of the history of art, Free University, Amsterdam, can help us understand the line at which the Christian must either accept or challenge any culture:

> It is basic to thinking about culture . . . that there is no duality between a higher and a lower, between grace and nature. This world is God's world. He created it, He sustains it, He is interested in it. He called the work of His hands good in the very beginning. Nothing is excluded. . . . yet there is a sharp division . . . between the Kingdom . . . of God, and the kingdom of darkness. Man, in the Fall brought sin and, consequently a curse into the world. And so there is a duality, between good and bad, right and wrong, beautiful and ugly . . . this is the true division.[8]

Now Dr. Rookmaaker specifies the Christian's proper attitude toward culture—"the very practical problem of how we are to live in a world that is full of sin and ungodliness." He explains:

> Where things are loving, good, right and true, where things are according to God's law and His will for creation, there is no problem. The Christian will appreciate and actively enjoy and enter into all the good things God has made. But where they have been spoilt or warped by sin, then the Christian must show by his life, his word, his actions, his creativity what God really intended them to be. He has been made new in Christ, been given a new quality of life which is in harmony with God's original intention for man. He has been given the power of God Himself by the Holy Spirit who will help him work out his new life into the world around him. He is the "salt of the earth," keeping society from corruption, and giving savour to every aspect of life.[9]

26

Perhaps this wise guidance will underscore the fundamental viewpoint of this book. *It is not to encourage a cultural approach to religion, but a religious approach to culture.*

The cultural approach to religion is one of our very real perils. Culture is not the door into the kingdom of God. Nicodemus doubtless had plenty of culture, but still needed to be born again. Evangelicals are in grave danger of becoming "culture-Christians."

The majority of our youth are not rebels. They are not "cop-outs." They see no need to defy the institution as a means of establishing their own identity. On the contrary, they have good rapport with their parents and the older generation in general. Many of their heroes are preachers and missionaries and their happiest memories relate to church-centered activities. They love the church and feel it is their own. They are accustomed to its peculiarities, even its restrictions, and have never developed any big hang-ups about them.

But in all of this, their religion may be only cultural. They may have missed the heart, which is knowing Christ. When such deluded youth get out of the church and home nest into an alien culture, their cultural religion will fail them. It will be weighed in the balances of the world's powerful pagan influences and will be found wanting. Public polish is no substitute for private piety; and equally, integration with our religious environment is not a substitute for union with Christ.

But while this is a real peril, the existential mood of our day confronts us with another illusion—that of supposing there is no connection between culture and religion. We imagine that we can be good Christians and look like radical revolutionaries. We think that if our morals are right no one has any right to criticize our life-style. But this is a pathetic —and I am bound to add, immature—misunderstanding. We cannot free culture from the authority of religion, if we are to be biblical; we ought not to try, if we want to be useful. And we won't *want* to try, if intelligent understanding is combined with genuine holiness of heart.

2

Our Culture Crisis

Everyone believes in culture, even those who pretend indifference. People will defend the culture in which they were born, or perhaps the subculture which they have elected to join. The same holds true for culture defined as improvement. No matter how crude or coarse a man may be personally, he believes in improved corn, frying chicken, automobiles, farm machinery, breeding stock, fruit trees, flowers, tools, building materials, and cooking—especially cooking. And it is astonishing how hippies, who profess to have copped out of the "establishment," still like good seats in fast jets and gladly accept rides in swank cars.

But while everyone believes in some form of culture, not everyone sees the importance of cultivating the self. In this slovenly and lawless age, refinement, manners, and good taste too often seem like vestiges from Noah's ark. It is time we awakened to the appalling barbarism which engulfs us. And it is time we saw not only our own cultural impoverishment, but the reduction of our Christian influence, and the consequent dishonor to our Lord.

True *culture* comes from within. We speak of the culture of the mind or soul as we would talk about the culture of pearls. This at once raises a very pertinent question. Is a "cultured" pearl real? Yes, for even though the nucleus is planted in the shell by man, the beautiful, lustrous gem still must be formed from within. What is to be feared in shopping for pearls is not the cultured kind but the imitation. These are glass beads, coated with "pearl essence," which is really no such thing, but a creamy liquid extracted from fish scales—shiny enough to fool the unwary.

This helps us to see that if we are going to aim at becoming cultured persons we must make up our minds whether we will settle for the false or go after the real. The synthetic variety is a lot easier to acquire, and looks quite authentic until people get close enough to scratch through the veneer. Unfortunately most people in our day have only a superficial culture. This is one reason ours is called a "plastic society."

CURRENT CULTURAL MOODS

While the emphasis in this book is on personal culture, we would do well to scan the moods and traits of modern Western society. We have distinguished between character and culture, yet now we must admit that our culture crisis is more fundamentally a character crisis. The culture crisis is but the outward manifestation of the moral decadence. This is the very reason Christians dare not permit their culture to be fashioned totally by the cultural moods around them.

We have been told repeatedly that ours is a secular society, shot through with materialism and hedonism. "The standard of living is the god of twentieth-century America and Europe and the adman is its prophet," writes Ronald J. Sider of Messiah College. The evidences are overwhelming.

The underlying secularism breaks out in ethical relativism, irresponsible individualism, and social rootlessness. There is a shocking lack of personal integrity and, equally, of a sense of community. The hedonism is seen in the "fun" mentality and the constant accent on "escape"—from the kitchen, the family, the job, the four walls. The current drug mania is a mark of that irresponsibility. The rootlessness is seen in our shortcuts and quickie attachments, and our ephemeral fads which rise and fall with our moods.

In *Understanding Media*, Marshall McLuhan has pointed out that the explosion of electronic mass media has shifted our way of thinking from the orderly and sequential patterns of the printed page to the diffuse and generalized stimulus of the picture. In this shift, a sense of history, of orderliness, of time, and of process tends to be lost, and as a consequence the "Now Generation" wants instant maturity, instant privilege, instant power, and instant change along with its instant coffee and potatoes.

To a bewildering degree the wheel, the transistor, the can, the thermostat, and disposable Kleenex are symbols of Western culture. We're on the road; we watch more than we read, and talk more than think. We are mass operators of mass-made machines and gadgets, but few of us are creative or inventive; still fewer are ingeniously resourceful. We suppose all we need to control life is sufficient knobs and push buttons, when in reality the knobs and push buttons are controlling us. We are not as concerned about durability as convenience and appearance. Whether it is styles, houses, cars, or jobs we are conditioned to change, including planned obsolescence. Unfortunately this conditioning spills over into our friendships and principles. What one professor of psychology calls "instant noninvolving intimacy" is especially characteristic of the "rock" culture.

But we pay dearly for our bouncy transience. Because we are shallow we are easily uprooted, easily estranged, easily diverted. We are less able to see things through with ingenuity and persistence. It becomes too easy for us to shed responsibilities. When obligations accumulate and problems multiply, we just move away from them.

One of the most debilitating forms of our decay is a loss of concern for excellence. We think quantitatively rather than qualitatively. We accept the shoddy as the norm. We have lost the character of the true artisan, who takes joyous pride in a job well done. Our satisfaction is no longer in our work, only in our paycheck. Yet even there "satisfaction" is a misnomer, for it is never enough to suit us.

Furthermore, we shy from the difficult, and take the easy way. A prominent contemporary musician commented in a recent radio interview that his little daughter, just beginning violin lessons, wasn't interested in learning how to hold the bow; she just wanted to play a tune. Of course! Desiring the pleasure of performance without the pain of such bothersome nonsense is a universal trait of children. Adults feel this way too, except that their maturity is seen in their adult insight that in real life we don't get to the top of the mountain without climbing, and that there is a relationship between such exciting things as playing tunes and such drab things as properly holding the bow.

When the father divulged the aversion of his daughter, the radio MC commented: "Perhaps that is the reason the guitar is so popular—it's easier." No comment could have been more of a bull's-eye. While a guitar mastered can be a vehicle of high art, as popularly used it is the symbol of our prevailing folk culture, which too often is the product of a lazy creativity. It is a creativity without toil, without thoroughness, without breadth or depth, without discipline —and therefore without excellence.

Not only have we lost the fine mettle of pride in our work and thoroughness in our masteries, but we have become a generation of litterbugs. A leisurely walk has long ceased to be a joy, for the omnipresent trash is so depressing that one feels physically ill. One wonders how human beings can so degenerate. A cartoon shows the Statue of Liberty almost buried by a mountain of bottles, cartons, and cans, with the lady of "liberty" announcing, "No deposit—no return!"

Another area of culture crisis is in the relationships between the sexes. Dr. James Dobson calls our attention to the widespread trend toward "unisex," which he defines as "the blending of the masculine and feminine roles." The lines are blurred between men and women. Women have become more aggressive, men more passive. Hairdos and dress are deliberately bisexual. "Historically," he says, "unisex attitudes have preceded the disintegration of societies which drifted in that direction." He quotes Dr. Charles Winick, professor of anthropology at City University of New York, as claiming that of the 55 cultures "characterized by sexual ambiguity" not one "has survived." As far as our present situation is concerned, Dr. Dobson believes that much of our current "homosexual epidemic" can be attributed to this culture trend.[1]

Because these trends relate not only to culture but to character, Christians should take an honest look at themselves. For too many manifest the same rootlessness and fly-by-night irresponsibility, the same restlessness with traditional roles, as their non-Christian contemporaries.

THE FINE ARTS JUNGLE

Two by-products of this cultural wilderness are, (1) a tragic fragmentation of society into subcultures, and (2) (surprisingly) an atrocious and sinister decadence in the realm of the fine arts. Never were more instruments bought, or fewer mastered; never more singers, or poorer voices; never more records sold, of worse bunkum and rubbish; never more lip service paid to culture, yet city after city is

33

finding it increasingly difficult to finance a symphony orchestra (in contrast to the huge sports complexes being built).[2]

It is no wonder that R. Murray Schafer declares that "before ear training it should be recognized that we require ear cleaning." In *The New Soundscape* he says:

> Together with other forms of pollution, the sound sewage of our contemporary environment is unprecedented in human history. . . . The time has come in the development of music when we will have to be concerned as much with the prevention of sounds as with their production.[3]

Perhaps no one has sketched more graphically the bottom dredging of our current cultural decadence in the fine arts than another critic, Marya Mannes. In a TV interview she said:

> There is a great new conspiracy afoot. You don't see any pickets or angry demonstrations for it, because the battle is almost won. The battle was to change just one little word in the U.S. constitution. Remember that phrase, "The pursuit of happiness"? Well, folks, it's now the pursuit of ignorance. Ignorance is not only bliss, it's a guaranteed right. . . .
>
> It flourishes in that new form of pollution called the counter-culture, glorious proof that never in any time in history has more junk been produced or more people bludgeoned into accepting it as art. The pursuit of ignorance is the pride of the new "natural man." Feel, don't think. Let it all hang out. Do your own thing. An artist is a man who calls himself one. Experience is bad for you. Knowledge is bad for you. The past is dead. The amateur is king. The less you know about something, man, the truer you are. And so on.
>
> So during the last decade, the counter-culture has produced, among thousands, the following phenomena: major museums have at different times exhibited such tokens of the new creativity as piles of dirt, crushed fenders, a mattress with the stuffing sprouting through and a melting toilet with a soiled rag in it. A proud possession

34

of Yale University is a monument of a giant lipstick that at least reflects our climate by combining an ABM missile with a public phallus. . . .

These countless doodles of the counter-culture are also the result of a generation brought up in the ugliness of our cities, having no close community with nature and no common standards of aesthetics. They have grown up blissfully ignorant of the English language. It is massacred daily by those who never bothered to learn its power, its beauty and its range. . . . The counter-culturists bombard us with what they like to call people's theatre, improvisations and explosions of bodies, obscenities, protests and symbols—called plays. . . .

We are not talking of the real talent, the real creators, born—thank heaven—in every age. A few manage to survive even now. But it remains to be seen whether a public deafened and battered by this climate of anti-reason and anti-mind, nurtured in ignorance and sold on fakers, will be able to tell the difference.[4]

Why is all this important to us as Christians? Because we are in danger of so accepting our junk culture that we become a part of it.

If we have been soundly regenerated, God has planted in our soul the beginning of the pearl; but unless we break away from the iron grip the world has on us, the pearl will never mature. For while God seeks to fashion us, the culture about us is fashioning us too, and the divine pearl is in grave danger of being crushed by the ruthless squeeze of a pagan society. This not only *can* happen; it *is* happening all the time. But when it happens we are useless as professed Christians. We may think that we are identifying with the world to win the world, but we are only surrendering our identity as redeemed and transformed children of God.

There are too many things about today's culture which are not just sub-Christian; they are anti-Christian. We cannot afford to wear the marks of anti-Christ. It is time for the appearance of some modern Shadrachs, Meshachs, and Abed-negos, who calmly but flatly announce to the old tyrant, "Be it known unto thee, O king, that we will not

35

serve thy gods, nor worship the golden image which thou
hast set up" (Dan. 3:18).

Escape from the Wilderness

We cannot find our way out of our cultural wilderness
unless we have some idea of how we got in. Penetrating
thinkers such as Francis Schaeffer, Harry Blamires, H. R.
Rookmaaker, and Addison Leitch are unanimous in pinpointing the gate. "Removing the absolutes," says Schaeffer,
"liberalism has led into a wilderness."[5] This is not only true
of ethics but of aesthetics. In rejecting the biblical revelation,
society "turned away from the total culture built upon that
truth, including the balance of freedom and form . . . a balance which has never been known anywhere in the world
before."[6]

The presupposition of the modern mind is that there
are no norms for art, no objective, authoritative standards,
no laws written in the nature of things—written by God—on
the basis of which it may be declared that this is good and
that is bad. A purely subjective approach prevails. Blamires
expresses it well: "Our culture is bedeviled by it's-all-a-
matter-of-opinion code"; and he predicts that the "words
true and *false* will eventually (and logically) be replaced by
the words *likeable* and *dislikeable*."[7]

Clyde S. Kilby writes as a *Christian* when he rejects
the willy-nilly chartlessness of pure subjectivism by saying:
"To believe in God involves accepting Him as the sovereign
perfection, not only of truth and goodness but also of
beauty, thus establishing the highest possible conceptions
of excellence."[8]

To "think christianly" (Blamires' phrase) we must see
that Christianity declares standards by which both societal
and personal culture can be judged. In declaring such standards its authority is divine revelation in Christ, in the Bible,
and also in the natural order, which reflects the will of God.

It is the duty of the Christian to find Christian norms, and permit these norms to govern every phase of culture. These are not Platonic "forms" or universals, but laws of coherence and symmetry written into the universe because they are expressions of the Creator's own nature. If all things were made by the Logos (the Word), we can expect the natural order to be in some sense a transcription of the orderliness and form of Christ, the Word. "A thoroughgoing subjectivism dismisses the drive to find meaning in art and life," writes Kilby. "Christianity, on the other hand, assumes meaning to be attainable. In aesthetics it presupposes the possibility of great art, lesser art, and non-art."[9]

In ethics we find these norms in the Scriptures. In aesthetics—in our use of form, sound, and color—we may not know fully what the norms are, but we believe they are there, and we have the urge to conform to them to the degree of our insight. As "absolutes" (if we may dare to use that term), these laws of form are not narrow limitations which smother creativity; on the contrary they make the highest freedom and creativity possible. But they determine the boundaries beyond which culture becomes ugly, destructive, and anarchic.

This is simply to say that what is right in composition, in interior decorating, in color schemes, in arrangements of rhythm and sound, is not entirely a matter of personal taste. The moment we say this or that is in *poor* taste we are conceding some kind of criterion which is above *personal* taste. "The assumption of a standard prevents dismissal of the problems of artistic taste with the remark, 'Well, I know what I like,'" says Kilby.[10] Of course there is great latitude within this Christian framework for variation of tastes which are truly *personal*, with the varied tastes equally *good*. What is here being denied is that all tastes are equally good simply because they are personal. "What I like" may be atrocious.

Nor is good taste entirely a matter of custom. No doubt

custom can condition the ear and the eye, so that inferior artifacts do not consciously jar, just as our ears can be conditioned to a piano that is out of tune. But this does not alter the fact that it is out of tune. Aesthetic rightness, then, is deeper than custom, opinion, or personal taste. Its norms are found outside of ourselves in the unwritten laws of God.

While directed primarily to the current rejection of authoritative norms in morality, the following comments by Addison H. Leitch are equally applicable to aesthetics. He writes: "We fail to see that the decision to evade value judgments is based on a value judgment, namely that value judgments are not good." It is as a professor that he says:

> We think we make no moral decisions for our students and yet we do indeed, after casting off Bach and Beethoven, da Vinci and Michelangelo, insist on another kind of music and art as better, or another approach to the same disciplines—sitting loose, for example, on absolutes—as better than what our elders taught us. But I claim that these decisions are judgments resting somewhere on absolutes, the insistence, for example that feeling is better than logic, that loving is better than law.
>
> How can one say "better" about anything unless he already has assumed a "best" as a point of reference?[11]

Suppose a Christian does have inferior artistic taste— so what? Is it a sin? Certainly not if it is mere ignorance. To be genuinely Christian does not mean that we must be carbon copies of some official standard in music or art—as, for instance, the requirement of some religious groups that only black cars and black garb are permitted. But poor taste *can* become an ethical matter, if the Christian becomes aware that (in Kilby's words) "his tastes may be lower than his best judgment or his conscience might dictate."

REWARDS OF GOOD TASTE

There is no way to blot out the distinction between harmony and discord, order and disorder, balance and imbalance, propriety and impropriety; and these distinctions are the canons of good taste. Good taste prefers harmony to disharmony, order to disorder, balance to distortion, propriety to impropriety. Some dress, manners, music, speech is *appropriate* to this or that activity, this or that purpose, this or that place; while other dress, manners, music, speech *is not.* Not only so, but good taste is sufficiently "exercised to discern good and evil" in the world of aesthetics, that it recognizes harmony, order, balance, and propriety. And by the same token, it recognizes their opposites. It is the ignorant, untutored person who doesn't know the difference.

And the perverse, twisted person can never really have good taste, for he has a bizarre affinity for discord, disorder, imbalance, and impropriety. The zanier and more outlandish it is, the better he likes it. But though this perverse reversal of preferences is natural to the sinful man, it is not natural to the holy man. If he is still afflicted with poor taste, it is due to ignorance, not willful perversity.

Rebels always miss the most exquisite pleasures of the senses. By defying law, they settle for junk, and junk doesn't give the same satisfaction as quality—at least to a normal mind. All of which means that those who deny any norms, any rule of law, in a misguided idolatry of individualism, will settle for anything that fascinates for the moment. But in so doing they cheat themselves of the finer pleasures which are the reward of nobler endeavor.

My wife and I had the pleasure of redecorating and furnishing an old house—old, but possessing that homeyness and dignity which make a house "decoratable." We were careful that the floor covering, wallpaper, and woodwork not only blended properly, but set just the right atmospheric tone. Then the placement of the furniture and the pictures came next. The exact rightness of the major things was determined rather quickly. For example, the big oil painting of the fjord in Norway had to hang above the fireplace.

But some decisions were tentative, then revised over several months. We had an oriental plaque hanging on one wall. We both felt uneasy about it, but didn't know what was wrong. Finally we took it down and put in its place a simple plate, and suddenly breathed a sigh of relief. We could have shouted, "*Eureka*—We have found it!" Another decision concerned a chair which had been placed in one corner, in a grouping of several items. One morning when I was trying to pray, it suddenly dawned on me that that chair didn't belong there; it needed to change places with the chair in the opposite corner. So my devotions were punctuated by some quick furniture moving. I tell you it was easier to pray afterward. I was adjusting the room to the "laws" of God. When my wife saw it she said, "Of course! Why didn't we see that before!" Now we were not inventing sound decorating; *we were discovering it.* Those formally trained or more experienced would have been able to see such misfits immediately, but we had to grope our way into rightness. *And each discovery brought us to a higher level of satisfaction.*

Like it or not, there are laws which operate in the aesthetic world, and there is an invisible court of justice which imposes a fine for their violation. The fine is deprivation of pleasure on a level which enriches and adds savor to life. Modern rebels in the world of art are paying this fine. But more seriously, the fine they are paying is the increment of coarseness. They live for the baser pleasures because they have settled for baser qualities in life. If men accept the mediocre and the inferior because they deny the essential laws of excellence, they will have to reap the dullness of mediocrity.

It becomes increasingly apparent, therefore, that for Christians to be indifferent to culture betrays a defective understanding of what it means to be thoroughly Christian. The naturalist and the humanist may attempt to be equally friendly to any form of culture simply because their philosophy presupposes man as the sole object, and nature (which in unsaved man is always degenerate nature) as the sole law. If it is "natural," it is right. If it is indigenous, it is right. But the Christian cannot go along. With the Christian, God is the object, not man. Man is in culture, but under God, and by God his culture is judged. The postulate of a Christian approach to culture must be that all cultural *norms* are derived from God. In his book *The Abolition of Man*, C. S. Lewis has argued convincingly that values can be discovered but not created, for they are part of ultimate reality.

We must repeat, therefore, that the obligation to be cultured is inherent in the Christian faith. It is an imperative which is second only to the command to be holy. Yet in a still deeper sense it is implicit in the command to be holy. For holiness includes putting our minds on the "lovely," the "lofty and whatever is praiseworthy," as well as the "true," the "just," and the "pure" (Phil. 4:8, Berkeley).

3

The Relation of Holiness and Culture

The title of H. Richard Niebuhr's book, *Christ and Culture*, might seem to give us the only proper reference point in a Christian approach to culture. If Christ is Truth, the "express image" of God and the revelation of His will, then He becomes the Norm for culture as well as ethics. All of life finds its meaning and vocation in Him. The facts of science must be interpreted by the Word, by whom all things were made. The artifacts of any society must find either their justification or their condemnation in Him.

Christ is the divine Touchstone which discovers the ethical implications in those so-called amoral things which were supposed to have no ethical implications. In Him culture and ethics surrender their independence, and are found to be, not unrelated, but complementary to each other. He shows the inner bond between what is right and what is proper, between good morals and good taste. Therefore a Christian who would understand his true relationship to his own culture and to the culture around him must never for one moment allow Christ to get out of focus.

Would it not be better then for this chapter to stick to Niebuhr's title, *Christ and Culture*? Is not the theme "Holiness and Culture" a detraction?—perhaps some kind of step-down?

THE REAL ENEMY

The full meaning of Christ for culture cannot be found in a consideration of His person alone, either as normative Man or as Son of God. In other words, if we would know how to judge culture and how to change it, either in ourselves or in society, we must not stop with the Incarnation, but must inquire into Christ's mission. Was it merely to show us by example what man should be? We know better than to turn into that cul-de-sac. It was rather to make available to man a power for becoming what he ought to be.

In that mission of Christ were both diagnosis and cure. The diagnosis was to pronounce man a sinner by choice and sinful by nature. The cure has its source in the atoning death and validating resurrection of Christ, and consists of being changed from a sinner by choice to a saint by choice, and from sinfulness in nature to holiness in nature.

This holiness is an inward conformity to Christ. It is having the "mind" of Christ (Phil. 2:5). It is having Christ "formed" in us (Gal. 4:19). It is to be changed into His "image from glory to glory" (II Cor. 3:18). In the holy heart is a spontaneous affinity for everything Christ is. What He loves we love. What He endorses we endorse. What He rejects we reject. His will is our will. Increasingly His revulsions become our revulsions and His pleasures become our pleasures.

We have known all along that this was the secret of

43

good ethics. What we now need to see is that it is the basis of good culture as well; indeed it is the very essence of any culture which can claim to be Christian. Holiness thus becomes a yardstick for evaluating culture, and the indwelling Holy Spirit becomes the indispensable Dynamic for the changing of culture—at least our own.

What we have not taken with sufficient seriousness in religious circles is that the great impediment to Christian enculturation is neither environment nor ignorance, but sin. By its very nature, sin is inherently anti-cultural, anti-intellectual, and anti-aesthetic. This explains why the popular movements of secular society almost always tend toward disorder and novelty and toward a breaking of norms. As a consequence, there is the exaltation of the coarse, the bizarre, and the sensual. This is true in literature, in art, in music, and in life-styles. The great performers and artists who have risen above the common level, and who have sought by their genius to elevate society, have been compelled to struggle against the strong undercurrents of decadence. They have mistakenly supposed that the explanation was in environment and ignorance, and that the remedy was in education and social reforms. Their dreams have repeatedly been dashed for the simple reason that the problem is deeper—it is in man's sinful heart.

CULTURE AND THE INNER MAN

Therefore the possibility of holiness becomes extremely relevant to the whole question of culture, whether societal or personal. To talk about holiness is not to shift the center of attention away from Christ. It is to bring Christ to bear upon the problems of culture fully rather than partially. For it can scarcely be overemphasized that the springs of good culture are in the heart more than in the head. In saying this there is the risk of seeming to be repetitious, but the importance justifies the risk. Inventive genius, artistic creativity, and technical know-how may be matters of the head and hand; but meaning, purpose, and use are of the heart. It is in cleansing the heart and residing in it as Lord and Master that Christ is supremely glorified. The concept of holiness directs our attention to this central glory of Christ's self-fulfillment in us.

From the Christian standpoint, therefore, culture as well as ethics is grounded in the inner man. A holy man has in him the essence of good culture just as he has in him the essence of goodness. But in so saying we are distinguishing sharply between the essence of culture and the externalities of culture. Just as a dedicated Christian may still have, unknowingly, ethical blind spots in his everyday life, so he may have cultural defects in his life-style. But the basis for correcting both the ethics and the life-style is the same—the impulse toward improvement which is in the Spirit-filled heart, with its underlying motive to please God. For instance, true courtesy is first an inner spirit, then gradually a learned etiquette. The learned etiquette alone is play acting; it is this kind of facade which prompts much of the bitter criticism directed at our society. But holiness insures us against mere play acting. The outward etiquette will be a true courtesy, because it will spring from love in the heart.

Now when we separate the inner springs of culture from the outward acquisition of its forms, we can see that we have not fallen into the trap of erasing the moral distinction between sin and error. Both ethical blind spots and cultural defects are errors, but need not be sin. Nothing said here must encourage us to suppose there is no qualitative difference in the sight of God between crude taste in music (for instance) and dishonesty. The latter can and should be corrected at once, by repentance and divine cleansing; the former may take some time to correct and in the process require formal training. Yet the original thesis remains: There is a closer, a more inward and organic connection between ethics and culture than most of us have been aware of.

45

And so we turn our attention to the fundamental question: In what ways will the holiness ethic contribute toward the full Christianizing of our culture?

The Basis for Integrity

First, by *breaking the world's enslavement*, so that Christ can have His full sway. In some cases this deliverance is dramatic in sound conversion; unfortunately, in other cases it is not in evidence at all even after a highly charged emotional experience of "sanctification." But something has misfired. If we are still slaves to every whim of fashion and to pagan life-styles, just because this or that is the "in" thing, then our religious exposure has not "taken." The command, "Be not conformed to this world" (Rom. 12:2), is translated aptly by Phillips, "Don't let the world around you squeeze you into its own mold." While this refers primarily to the spirit of the world, it also includes the fashions and values shaped by that spirit. A world-squeezed Christian is still in bondage to the world, and as such does not yet experience the power of the Holy Spirit which emancipates.

A Spirit-filled person is not indifferent to the changes in moods and fads and fashions, but he enjoys a grand freedom. His stylishness will be modified by Christian principles, not controlled totally by social pressure. It is this inner freedom which makes him malleable into something new and different, as the Holy Spirit proceeds to lead him. Then we will observe a rich individuality and colorful uniqueness. A shrewd evangelical college student commented that "mold-making is much more acute among those who rebel than those who try to be the best possible persons."

Second, *holiness will prevent cultural phoniness*, by making us real persons within. We will inwardly be what we want people to think we are. We are told that ours is a plastic culture—artificial, unreal; a culture of substitutes. But the culture is plastic because the people are. People are plastic

46

because they are not pliable in the hands of God. When God shapes us it is into real persons, not into synthetic pretenders.

The Urge for Excellence

Third, by its very nature our union with Christ *creates in us a passion for improvement*. This has been noted already but needs to be looked at carefully. There is now a fire burning, an impetuous drive to glorify God. Zeal replaces apathy (Titus 2:14). The holy man knows why he is here, and what his aims are. He is no longer rambling at loose ends, for he has made the great presentation of Rom. 12:1, and will act accordingly. He will be galvanized into single-minded dedication to the all-embracing vocation of serving God. Very quickly the Holy Spirit will begin shaping him into some degree of coherence. It needs to be shouted from the housetops that love for God is not a gushy sentiment or dreamy ideal, but a powerful dynamic for the whole of life.

But to want to glorify God is to want to learn how. This implies desiring to acquire that competence as a person which will glorify God to the maximum of our potential. Such a Christian will not be content with mediocrity. This casualness which is in the atmosphere today, this sloppiness which pretends to be "natural," to live freely without the artificial conventions of society, to "let it all hang out" as Marya Mannes puts it, is really about 95 percent laziness. It is precisely the kind of laziness which prompts a child to sweep the dirt under the rug, or to fail to wash behind his ears. But holy living will cure sloth. Christian love is too dynamic, too driving and energizing for laziness to find a serious foothold. It will infuse us with a deep sense of responsibility.

This passion for improvement is radically different from a passion for winning. Competition may have its place,

47

but if mere competitiveness is the whole of our drive, if this is what makes us go, we are indeed to be pitied, for this is so futile and destructive. One young man confessed to the writer that for years he did his best in everything only because he couldn't stand being second. For him energetic striving was not healthy but feverish, for he was being lashed by the whip of a sick ego. But when love for God conquers this self-centeredness, we find ourselves desiring to do our best, not just to beat someone, or to be praised, but for Jesus' sake.

This passion for improvement is the best safeguard against cheapness. Because we are surrounded by low aims, low standards, low advertising appeals, and hence cheap people, we are in constant danger of being cheap ourselves. A cheap person is one whose values are cheap. He stops growing too soon. He settles for trashiness in entertainment, language, and appearance, when he could have quality.

It may not necessarily be evidenced in torn jeans, uncombed hair, and street jargon. We have put a low ceiling on our growth just as pathetically when our value system rises no higher than sports cars or flashy clothes. Here is a girl whose sole goal in life, apparently, is to get attention, and whatever brains or talent or money she has is exhausted on herself, in wild hairdos and glamorous eye makeup and daring dress, while her Bible is neglected, her office work suffers, or her grades decline. This girl is cheap though she knows it not. Likewise the young male who gets more satisfaction out of burning rubber than out of a good deed or a good book is showing his age—his mental age, that is. If he settles on that level he will be a cheap person, for he has sold himself short.

But the passion for improvement which is intrinsic to holy living will not permit us to be cheap persons. This is no guarantee that we will suddenly have old heads on young shoulders, but it is a guarantee that the young heads as well as old heads will be in earnest about the serious business of life.

Our True Humanness

Fourth, in that inner purity which is the gift of Christ *we find our true humanness*. We are not supermen, but restored men—not just as we were in childhood, but more like man was intended to be in the beginning. In our minds, bodies, and personalities there are yet many scars and lingering vestiges of our twisted humanness. But we have seen in Christ what it means to be normally human, and we are inwardly conformed to what we have seen.

This means that the traits which belong to essential humanity belong to us. Briefly, they are as follows:

a. A spontaneous affinity for God as the supreme value. A normal man is a God-centered man.

b. An inner harmony with ourselves. A normal person is not engaged in a civil war.

c. A creative at-homeness with the environment of the natural order. We are clay as well as spirit; creatures of the earth and sky, and sights and sounds, as well as the trysting walk with God in the cool of the day.

d. We experience love for our fellows. We are constructively related to our own kind.

All of this was true of the first Adam before the Fall, and it was true of the Second Adam. It can be true of us.

This four-sided relationship which is essential to normal humanness is a unity. Disruption at any point results in a disturbance of the whole. There has been a disastrous, devastating disruption on a racial scale. Man has lost his normal humanness and as a result is both alien to his Father's world and a stranger to himself, not knowing his true identity. In hiding from God he has become lost from himself. As C. S. Lewis puts it, "Spirit and Nature have quarrelled in us; that is our disease."[1]

Being estranged from God, man is also estranged from his fellows, hence his shocking "inhumanity to man," his abnormalities and perversions, his monstrous selfishness. In his relation to the natural order he gropes for a lost concord. In the arts he reaches for the harmony which he fleetingly glimpses, but can only partially grasp. All his efforts are tarnished by the Great Dislocation. Since he cannot banish it from his soul he cannot keep it out of his community life, his technology, his arts and crafts. Across his beauty is the shadow of ugliness. Across his unity is the mockery of disunity. Alongside his nostalgic longing for harmony is at the same time that contradictory and irrational bent to disharmony and decadence.

Now this man—this dislocated man—will fashion a culture which reflects his dislocation. It may be Oriental or Western; it may be primitive or highly developed—all of which is relatively inconsequential. The important thing is that it will betray, throughout, the tension which now plagues him. As Spirit-filled persons, we are so inwardly restored to the original fitness of things, the original harmonies of our true humanness, that we are searching for a culture which expresses this. And because our affinities are now so radically changed we cannot be completely at home in a culture which is impregnated through and through with the tangents and irregularities of the Great Dislocation.

It is inevitable therefore that the true Christian, especially when he is also highly cultured, will find himself much of the time at odds with the sin-shaped culture around him. Because of God's grace, and because of positive Christianizing influences in Western society for almost two millennia, that culture is not totally alien. Even so, it is still too pockmarked with the disease of sin to suit the Christian. As a consequence he will either tend to withdraw into a more congenial subculture or he will be challenging the culture around him in order to change it. He will appreciate some things, but reject others. Even within particular disciplines—

possibly drama or music or athletics—he will discriminate as a Christian. There will be sharp lines defining the limits of his approval and participation.

In summary we can say: Culture is no proof of a holy life. We may be cultured rogues. Neither is culture an acceptable substitute for holiness. But it can, and must, become an expression of the changed life. It is this relation to the holiness ethic which gives to culture its importance for the Christian. If we profess to be Spirit-filled yet identify comfortably with an incompatible and contradictory culture, we create an unbearable and indefensible dichotomy, which in the end will destroy both us and our witness.

4

Much Ado About Something

Good character is, of course, more important than good manners. Better to be pure than merely polished, to have a clear conscience than a trained voice, to have integrity than finesse in the social courtesies. But it doesn't have to be either/or. Why not both purity *and* polish? If we have a Christian view of things, we will not be content with a character which stops at ethical soundness and fails to include cultural accomplishments. Only as we are both good *and* gracious will we "give the light of the knowledge of the glory of God in the face of Christ Jesus" (II Cor. 4:6). Therefore this chapter concerns the *acquirement* of Christian culture.

If we desire a pearl culture rather than synthetic, in order that we may best glorify God and perhaps influence the prevailing culture around us, we must know the areas of our deficiency, and the direction we must take for improvement.

It may be surprising to some, perhaps even disappointing, that I shall not point in the direction of advanced degrees in education or years of concentration in music or art. This would be getting the cart before the horse. These avenues are not open to all, but the essential culture of soul is. In fact, overemphasis on formal education and the fine arts can develop a compartmentalized person who even in his accomplishments misses the essence of inner refinement. The artist, for instance, may be the most disorganized, undisciplined, and cluttered soul in the block.

EXCELLENCE AND TRIFLES

The most typical failure among people, and especially Christians, in becoming cultured is their failure to see the importance of details, and as a consequence a general slovenliness of life-style is still too common. We need to be shocked out of our lethargy by the declaration of Oswald Chambers that "slovenliness is an insult to the Holy Ghost." The reason is not hard to guess. Slovenliness reflects a lazy unconcern about the very details which create either a Christian or a hippie image—and our image has a lot to do with our influence and our usefulness. A favorite teacher used to say, "Trifles make perfection, but perfection is no trifle." By trifles she meant details which looked like trifles to the immature mind but in reality were anything but trifling.

We are bound to admit, of course, that some details *are* trifles. They are petty and inconsequential, not worthy of a large share of anxiety. The ability to distinguish between small matters which are actually trivial and those which are not, especially in respect to Christian culture, is not just a question of intelligence, but of the degree to which we have acquired what Harry Blamires calls the "Christian Mind" in contrast to the secular mind. What the worldling classifies as trifling these days includes a great deal indeed—petty thievery, "white" lies, legal evasions. In fact there are many voices insisting that legal marriage is a mere trifle; only love

53

is important. Of course if we are Christians at all we know better than to follow the world this far; yet many of us are still hung up with the notion that if we just pay attention to the real big things the little things don't matter—that they are "much ado about nothing." We apply this not so much to areas plainly ethical as to those little things which have a subtle but profoundly significant bearing on culture. Let us then take a look at some of these little things to see how big they are.

Even vocationally our prospects are determined by our capacity for detail. This is true for the doctor, the accountant, the professor, the scientist, the architect, the engineer, or the minister. Disregard of detail will put a low ceiling on one's accomplishments. But how much more is this true in Christian culture! Negatively, it is "the little foxes that spoil the vines," and positively it is the little graces that make for excellence.

Every wife understands this. The margin between a so-so husband and one who fulfills her dreams lies in those little touches of perception, his thoughtfulness and consideration and understanding, the little looks and words which coarser souls never think about. To her, these tiny extras, beyond the bare minimum of staying sober and making a living, are the most important for her emotional happiness, for they seem to her to express the difference between nominal love and fervent love. She remembers how meticulous he was about detail when he was courting her, and she cannot be entirely content with a marriage in which those finer elements are forgotten.

This also is the key to the social grace which we call tact. Someone has defined tact as a sense of touch. But this kind of touch is a sensitive, delicate thing. It is spiritual perceptiveness, a sort of interpersonal radar, which picks up signals not seen or heard by ingrown egotists. Some people have no radar mechanism, or if they do it is almost chronically out of order. As a consequence they miss the finer

54

shadings, those peculiar nuances and tones of a situation, without which there can be no insight.

Most people would at least give lip service to the value of tact. But we need to see that it is the very essence of good manners, courtesy, even formal etiquette. Good manners smooth out the rough spots in human relations. For the Christian, politeness is not a device for getting something he wants; it is an expression of love and respect. It is a mark of Christian sensitivity. Henry Drummond reminds us that politeness is "love in trifles." The rage these days in some quarters is so-called "sensitivity training" (or more recently, "encounter culture"), much of which is more like *sensuality* training. But the Holy Spirit is the best Sensitivity Trainer we can have, if we will first cultivate sensitivity to Him. He will give us compassion and the inner capacity for empathy. He will make us aware of human needs around us, and will give us a feeling for the feelings of others, so that we desire not to hurt and embarrass needlessly.

With this attitude we will want to learn the art of courtesy. In learning the art we will include the *rules* of etiquette, whether civilized table manners or correct posture or how to dress when taking the offering in church. For the rules are not arbitrary whims dreamed up by Mr. and Mrs. Stuffed-Shirt. Just as the rules of grammar for the most part reflect the logic of language, so does good etiquette reflect the logic of true courtesy. As such the rules give shape and guidance to the impulse to be polite and gracious.

We learn propriety, for one thing. There are levels of dignity which belong to different occasions, and each level must be given its appropriate accessories of dress and conduct. An outdoor picnic is supposed to be informal. But dining indoors should rarely be turned into a rowdy picnic. Nor should church ushering be done in hiking clothes. As laughter is not suitable at a funeral, so honky-tonk music is not appropriate for a wedding. These are self-evident truisms when our attention is called to them; yet many thoughtless people either forget or do not love God and people enough to bother to learn how to avoid being crude and outlandish. The exhibitionist who enjoys being freakish is mentally juvenile, to say the least.

Let us now take a look in another direction. In the last few years we have been made increasingly aware of the deplorable pollution of our environment. The word "ecology" has been an "in" word. This is good; and sanctified people surely have a ready response to this. For, as was pointed out in the last chapter, one of the facets of our true humanness is a sense of at-homeness in the natural order. This means more than an appreciation for its beauties; it means a sense of the sacramental in the earthly. This world is God's gift, washed with color and pulsating with life, absolutely prodigal in abundance; for our physical needs, yes, but for our souls too. It is an avenue of communion with God. Every sanctified person ought to feel therefore a personal affront, a moral indignation, at the prostitution of this gift of God.

But here again we must insist that it is the detail that counts, and especially at the personal and individual level. Some years ago when Earth Day was celebrated, a sign was seen on a California campus: "We the people are the environmental problem." And so we are; not just the factories belching out smoke, but we as individuals littering our streets, and allowing our little patch of earth to become a disreputable trash heap.

In many ways the crudity of our unredeemed barbarism shows through. A young couple moved into a college-owned apartment the day after the previous occupants, just having graduated, moved out. The apartment had been left in an incredibly filthy condition. They may have graduated but they were not educated. Neither had their "holiness" reached a practical dimension. For cleanliness is still next to godliness, and dirt and dedication do not jibe. A good "brand" of holiness would have created impulses toward

56

order, neatness, and beauty. Moreover, holiness would have prompted them to think of those who were to follow them. There is nothing more practical in God's universe than heart holiness. Its promptings are toward homes, not pigsties; soap, not dirt; neatness, not disarray; beauty, not ugliness.

This carries over to the larger context. If truly honored, the Holy Spirit will shake the thoughtlessness out of the litterbug, and will convict the industrialist about needless spoilage of waters, forests, and air. In the meantime, in our little corner it is hypocritical for us to write essays on the ecological sins of the industrialist if our own houses are a shambles and our yards look like a ballpark after the game, or like Main Street on the morning after the hurricane. Ecology, like charity, begins at home.

A Mark of Maturity

The above illustrations underscore the importance of detail in several of the more noticeable areas of life. It is easy to think of applications in other areas. Yet these finer details of excellence are apt to be the very things that some types of mentality laugh at, as being "Mickey Mouse."

Admittedly, the "now" generation has a point when it reacts against the kind of culture which is all window dressing. Many young people have grown up in homes where every ounce of energy was exhausted on appearances —a "keeping up with the Joneses" sort of thing. But behind the glittering showcase there were no goods—no real love, no real honesty, no real compassion, certainly no real happiness. Children soon sense this discrepancy; then by the time adolescence is reached the sheer hollowness of it strikes them full in the face. It is small wonder if in a pathetic and misguided search for genuineness they sometimes rebel and "cop out."

Fortunately there are the many sensible young people who have enough wisdom to reach up and grasp the pendulum before it swings from one extreme of sham to the other. They know that smashing the showcase isn't going to put goods on the shelves. It is better to leave the showcase intact but go to work to justify it. It is a very immature mind that thinks to avoid the emptiness of their elders they must throw out the niceties and amenities of civilized living along with the hypocrisies. They suppose that getting back to "nature," as they call it, is the same as getting back to depth and decency of character. It isn't anything of the sort. It isn't combs, soap, barbershops, and shoebrushes which are the symbols of decadence but a lot of other things, such as drugs, rock festivals, and—yes, the pill.

Isn't it odd that the young people who are the most vociferous in their rejection of the refinements of civilization are very commonly the very ones who fall for the vices. They despise such knowledge as arranging table placings properly and dressing formally, but they know all the tricks of "making out." To avoid being mannequins they become scarecrows. One wonders if while trying to escape the artificialities of civilization they have in spite of themselves fallen heir to the hypocrisy. At least they have failed to discern between the vanities of secular civilization and the virtues of common civility.

Now how is this relevant to us—*today*? Simply in the fact that most of us have been more or less affected by the temper of the times. As Christians we reflect more strongly the virtues—the quest for genuineness and the social concerns—but we are also infected, at least ever so slightly, by this generation's special shams and fictions. The disposition to discount appearances and scorn little details of good manners is one example. If anyone tells us to watch our posture, or to use good English, or to observe table manners, or dress appropriately, we think they are being fussy. These things are, in our "emancipated" view, unimportant; they just don't matter. But they do matter, far more than we know.

58

Two gospel singers could be named who have almost equal voices, but greatly disparate impact. What makes the difference? The answer is in their bearing on and off the platform, the way they sit, the way they stand, how they handle their hands. In the one man what you see is as pleasing as what you hear; in the other, you enjoy the voice better if you shut your eyes.

Or take this example. A minister was negotiating with a church about becoming their pastor. In the end they did not call him. The reason may seem petty; it was because of carelessness in the wording of one of his letters. The board became suspicious that he lacked scholarship, and upon investigation their suspicions were confirmed. One who knew him well commented: "Mr. ——— is gifted with a glibness of utterance which in his earlier years he mistook for real ability. As a consequence, he has never held in high esteem that true scholarship which alone can build a strong ministry. I fear he is being heavily smitten with disappointment in these later years."[1]

Acting the Part

There is a powerful argument for carefulness in cultural detail which has not yet been mentioned. I refer to the psychological law of response to role playing. Much is said these days among educators about the action-reflection model of learning. This means (according to the theory) that we learn best by doing first, then reflecting on it afterward. As a pedagogical issue I will not debate the matter. But there is in character building and behavior shaping a similar principle, the validity of which can be vouched for. We might call it the behavior-character model. We tend to conform inwardly to the image we assume outwardly. We have said that if you are a gentleman you will act like one. That is true, but the reverse is also true. If you act like a gentleman you are very apt to become one; unless, of course, the process is

59

blocked by a deliberate ulterior motive. But the principle is observable in most cases. Dress like a tramp and you will tend to think like a tramp and act like one. Dress up and your conduct spruces up too. For if you do not respect yourself and others in the way you dress you will not respect yourself or others in the way you act.

There seems to be a psychological power of suggestion here, that when you put on symbols of certain kinds of character, the matching behavior is triggered quite subconsciously. Eula May Miller refers to a famous folk singer who says he likes his wife with dirty, stringy hair because dirt brings out the animal nature in one![2] This may explain why people will do things at a masquerade party, for instance, that they would never dare to do in normal circumstances. And this is why a certain high school coach insists that his team dress in their "Sunday best" when travelling—"They behave better." Dress can either serve as a guardian of our inhibitions or as a thief of our inhibitions. But when our inhibitions go, our character goes too. As Will Durant has said, "Inhibition—the control of impulse—is the first principle of civilization."[3]

Casualness is proper at times, but the trouble is we have made it a fetish. Whether shopping or going to school or even to church, we take too literally the invitation of the second-class hotel, "Come as you are." And the sloppier we come, the sloppier we tend to act. A slouch in the body is a pretty good sign of a slouching mind. The principle here is: In some roles in life we begin by acting the part; then our feelings and attitudes follow along. If we want to be alert, intelligent, and up-and-coming people, we begin by looking and acting like that kind of persons.

A Quality of Grace

When we weave together the various threads of what has been said in this chapter, we will find that it is not too far removed from what God's Word means in II Pet. 3:18, where we are told to "grow in grace." A friend commented that the old Fort Garry Hotel in Winnipeg ought to be preserved because the public rooms have that "rare quality of grace" found so often in the older architecture but so seldom in the new. Instantly I thought of some of the rooms and buildings which I had seen, which in addition to their functional practicality had that beauty, warmth, and dignity called grace. The little mountain cabin of Miss Alice, described in Catherine Marshall's novel *Christy*, had it. So it isn't money that makes the difference.

But most important, all of us can think of people who have this grace. There is about them a graciousness of spirit and manner not to be confused for one moment with artificial and affected mannerisms. It is the product of the molding, refining influences of the Holy Spirit. God designs that His grace within become graciousness without. This is what Oswald Chambers meant by the statement: "Not only must our relationship to God be right, but the external expression of that relationship must be right."[4] This is the translation of inner holiness into total gentleness and refinement. Indeed what better description of graciousness could there be than the fruit of the Spirit—"love, joy, peace, longsuffering, gentleness, goodness, faith, meekness, temperance" (Gal. 5:22).

We then become like those rare buildings which have grace. When this happens we unconsciously create an atmosphere which affects people who come within our orbit of influence. Quite simply and naturally, they are being drawn into the magnetic field of our Lord's grace. You see, the right kind of culture is also a kind of evangelism.

5

The Christian's Cultural Tensions

When we begin to fashion life to a pattern that is both normally human and biblically Christian, some apparent tensions will disturb us. But in our efforts to resolve these we will find that that which is the most biblically Christian is the most normally human. At the deepest level there is no real clash between the claims of good culture and the demands of the Spirit-filled life. But in the adjustment period of our Christian walk we do not yet fully perceive this unity. It is like typing: at the level of mastery the method of typing which is technically correct is also the easiest and most natural. But during the agony of learning, it seems anything but. In piano playing also, correct fingering is really the easiest and most natural way to play—but not always for the beginner.

We cannot overemphasize the truth that true Christian

living does not create either abnormality or eccentricity. It is rather a life of true holiness which includes the whole man and makes the whole man whole. It weds heavenly-mindedness with earthly-mindedness. It insists on the priority of good churchmanship, but within the context of good citizenship. Above all, it tends toward healthy-mindedness as persons; not necessarily persons who are well in body, but who are balanced, wholesome, and constructive in outlook.

Such a person is a far cry from the religious juggler who tries to balance neatly the claims of godliness over against the pull of worldliness, and ends up with a nauseating blank for both sides. True holiness is all-embracing. It cleanses, then assimilates every normal element of human life, including our conjugal and social relationships, vocations, life-style, the physical side of life as well as the religious and intellectual. But in its very demand for absolute totality, holiness both uncovers and resolves some cultural tensions. Let us look at some of them.

A World Enjoyed Versus a World Renounced

Augustine was entirely right in teaching that the true object of enjoyment is God. But he was wrong in concluding that therefore this world was not to be enjoyed. That the *world spirit* or worldly spirit is to be rejected is undeniable, but at the moment we are using "world" in the sense of the natural order of which we are a part. Even this must not be the primary object of our affection—that would be idolatry. But it can be highly esteemed as a reminder of its Creator, whom we love supremely.

Enjoyment of a dear friend is first of all in his personal presence. But there are secondary sources of enjoyment which are very precious and real—perhaps a letter from him, or his picture, or a treasured gift from his hands. Whatever reminds us of our friend gives us joy because it represents him. So likewise the Christian whose happiness is supremely in God will be the very one who will most enjoy the earthly blessings which he perceives to be gifts from God. All things beautiful will quicken his devotion. Even the lovely and skillfully wrought artifacts of culture will prompt praise to the God who so magnificently shared His own creativity with man.

The fact that "the whole world [of men] lieth in wickedness" (I John 5:19) does not make us traitors when we look for those values in creation which remain unspoiled. Because sinful pleasures are forbidden we are not to think it pious to shun legitimate pleasures, for God "giveth us richly all things to enjoy" (I Tim. 6:17—written from *prison*, no less!). And even those gifts which have been tarnished by sin, such as marriage and friendship, can be purified, so that their enjoyment is once more wholly in God and wholly without sin. This too is the message of holiness.

Nothing is more compatible with righteousness than a sensitive aliveness to the beautiful. When the soul is filled with God, the aesthetic needs are more readily met, and on a more authentic and healthy level. Cultured people who are also deeply Christian find exquisite pleasure in the simple beauties of life, such as the delicacy of china, the fragrance of flowers, the wonder of cascading clouds. In contrast, worldly-minded people are apt to be too sin-jaded to be satisfied with such simple objects at hand. Instead, they restlessly seek the artificial excitements of the garish and glamorous. Without God, beauty only tantalizes the deeper longing. Artificial excitements then compound the frustration. As a result the poor sinner, alienated from God, is wearied by the vicious cycle created by his own discontent.

It should not be supposed, however, that one's enjoyment of this world must be confined to the beauties of nature and invention. The true Christian shares with God His love for men also. And in this love there is some degree of simple, unembarrassed liking for people as people. This wonder and excitement in people transcends their moral worthiness or spiritual condition. We should know how to enjoy people simply because all of us share in a common humanity.

This does not imply indifference to the evil of men, or a complacency with people as they are. We will love them as God loves them, first as the created image of himself, and second as the subject of His redemptive sufferings. This will make our love costly, and blend enjoyment with tears and delight with grief—sometimes anger. But too often we have had the anger for the sinner and reserved the enjoyment for the saint. In a sense this is natural and inevitable, for the saint is our spiritual kin while between us and the sinner is a gulf of spiritual alienation. We hesitate to bridge this gulf because the same gulf exists between him and God, and we choose to be on God's side. But in taking God's side it is easy to call down fire from heaven on wicked men, and thus fail to be *like* God, who makes the sun shine and the rain fall on them all.

The plea here is very simple: Not only an evangelistic love belongs to holy living, but a very earthy love of people as fellow human beings. Perhaps our evangelistic love would be more effective, and seem less professional, if we had a little more artless, unguarded, no-contest-to-win enjoyment in people as people. In spite of the defacement of sin, the wonder of man should entrance us at least as much as the wonder of stars.

INDIVIDUALISM VERSUS CONFORMITY

Then there is the tension between *individualism* and *conformity*. This is the conflict between so-called "rugged individualism" and spineless echoism (the "me too" response to life). The slogan of the would-be individualist is, "I want to do my own thing." The supreme aim of the conformist is to "get with it." The irony is that generally the self-styled individualist is the most complete conformist. It so happens that breaking molds is fashionable in our day, so because this self-advertised "individualist" feverishly wants to be in step, he conforms to the cult of nonconformity. A recent cartoon in *Saturday Review* showed a typical hippie confronting a typical businessman with the words, "Father—Oh, I beg your pardon, Sir; I thought you were my father. You all look alike, you know." Of course the humor is in the hippie imagining that he is an individualist while his father is a conformist. It seems that the pot never learns not to call the kettle black. Actually, most of us are more conformists than we are individualists, self-delusions otherwise notwithstanding. The difference is in our drum majors. Some conform to majorities, others to minorities; some to the "in" thing, others to the "out"; some to the new, others to the old; *and*—much more seriously—some to Christ, others to the world.

The Christian view of life sees that as to individualism and conformity, each has its proper due. It is the lopsided overemphasis which is dangerous and anti-Christian. Freedomistic philosophies, such as existentialism, exaggerate individualism. Freedom is the watchword, and personal autonomy is the aim. On the other hand, totalitarian philosophies and ideologies, such as Communism, stress conformity. Obedience is the watchword, and personal subjugation is the aim. Both exaggerations are diseases of the human spirit, and lead to the destruction of normal humanness.

On the one hand, unbridled individualism destroys the fabric of the social order. This is what Blamires calls "the atomism of anarchic individualism which has destroyed the cohesive forces which ought to discipline our social, cultural and national life."[1] If there is to be community, there must be some degree of conformity. Extreme individualism is thus anarchic and egoistic. It is childish rebellion—"No one is going to tell me what to do." The ultimate end is isolation and terrifying loneliness.

Such a pathological individualist cannot adjust to a

wife or husband, so there is one divorce and remarriage after another. He cannot adjust to the regulations of a job and cannot abide a boss over him. Every rule is seen as an infringement of his rights. So he spends his life protesting the oppressiveness of the "establishment," all the while drifting from one job to another. But in his senseless search for "freedom" he does not find peace; rather, he experiences only deepening unrest, bitterness, and despair. He is becoming a lonely island, and is rapidly destroying all bridges of common obligation and communication. Even his friends (if he has any at all) cannot in the end reach him in his self-made prison of rigid nonconformity. This is selfishness "gone to seed."

On the other hand, excessive lust for conformity is equally devastating. The person who wants above all to be a carbon copy of his "set" is perilously close to being a nonperson. He cannot tolerate the embarrassment of being the least out of step. He does not have the courage to break molds, even when he knows he is trapped in a mold which *ought* to be broken. The word "peculiar," as found in Titus 2:14 (KJV), makes him frightfully nervous. As the mood of the mass-mind, in fads and fashions, sways up and down and in and out, he sways with it.

This, of course, is exactly the kind of mentality Communism wants, for such a person can easily be brainwashed. He has already been brainwashed by the advertising media a dozen times; one more time will be no problem at all. Since totalitarian systems cannot tolerate deviation or private opinion, total submissiveness is the supreme virtue. In the end we have masses of subhuman robots, controlled by a few mastermind overlords.

We must have sufficient *individualism* to preserve the integrity of the person. We must have sufficient *conformity* to achieve community. How can we integrate the claims of both, and avoid the futile deadend extremes of either? Christian holiness is our answer, for it will emancipate a man

67

from the bondage of the mob, yet keep him under the discipline of God. It will teach him to find the true freedom of a synthesis between his integrity as a person and his duty as a unit of society.

Recently I listened to—and watched—a great symphony orchestra, backed by a 300-voice chorus. As I enjoyed the concert the thought came to me: Here is the answer to the question, How can I be free to be myself and still serve? That night I saw the true synthesis of individualism and conformity. In the great variety of instruments and voices, and the corresponding varieties of lines and parts, each person was richly, satisfyingly doing "his own thing." Yet he was doing it in such a way that his "own thing" was making a unique contribution to the total harmony, instead of being a jarring, destructive discord. How could this be? Because everyone's "own thing" found its common purpose and meaning in a common work of music performed under a common director. The result was composition—harmonious and beautiful —on a massive, soul-moving scale.

This is a parable of life. The synthesis of individualism and conformity which those musicians accepted in order to produce an evening of glorious music is the synthesis the holy man accepts for the whole of life, with Christ as the Conductor. When the self usurps the podium, we have the divisive destructiveness of unbridled individualism. When the state (or even "our crowd") is allowed the baton, we have the mindless goose-stepping of inordinate conformity. But when God is deliberately given His rightful place and followed carefully in His every direction, we have neither ugly individualism nor flat conformity. The result is colorful individualism and cooperative conformity in a perfect fusion of strength, usefulness, and beauty.

In the best sense, the most stimulating individualists are the saints, and at the same time it is the saints who are the happiest and freest conformists. Their will is yielded to God, and because it is yielded it is their own in the enjoyment of that liberty which by love serves one another (Gal. 5:13). They surrender their self-sovereignty, and, lo!—they are the only ones that have it!

Creativity Versus Conservatism

Next, we should face up to the tension between *creativity* and *conservatism*. Here again living under the lordship of Christ helps us first to be acutely aware of the problem, and then to resolve it. For both creativity and conservatism have legitimate claims, just as do individualism and conformism. Both are needed in the composition of a balanced Christian culture. But creativity leads to change; conservatism resists change. How are these apparently opposite impulses to be reconciled? Only by harnessing them both to a single master motive. Within that harness they learn to mutually respect the rights of the other. It is only when either becomes independent that it becomes destructive.

Creativity in itself is a God-given gift which is fundamental to our true humanness. It is the faculty which, by utilizing imagination, makes innovation and improvement possible. This becomes a menace to stability only when directed by the carnal mind, which is not subject to the law of God. The carnal mind creates a fever in the creative impulse and injects a desire to create without discipline, without rule, without norms. It makes us want to experiment not only legitimately, but in defiance of the laws of God; not only to invent new forms, but to break all the old molds. In the restless unhappiness of the sinful mind is a resentment of restrictions imposed as norms or absolutes. The evidence of this kind of anarchic creativity is a childish attempt to cut loose from the voice of the past and from the restraint of contemporary conventions. In the end, this kind of creativity creates nothing but chaos. Its beauty becomes cheaply glamorized ugliness and its forms become grotesque and ghoulish.

The indwelling Holy Spirit preserves and enhances the true creative instinct by cleansing us from the anarchic tendency. Then we can be free to be intelligent enough to see that beauty is to be found within the framework of God's order. Not only so, but He will sanctify our creativity by directing it into the service of God and humanity. The carnal mind desecrates creativity by prostituting it to the service of self; holiness restores creativity to its original intent—the glory of God.

But conservatism must also have its due. Every creative person has within his nature a conservative counterpart. One impulse of normal conservatism is a desire for the preservation of the loved and the familiar, whether that be people, things, customs, or places. This environmental stability is, in the natural, our strongest ally for mental health and contentment. To disturb this excessively by too many changes over too short a period of time is to invite emotional disturbance—sometimes even complete disorientation. This is the peril confronting America right now which Alvin Toffler discusses so alarmingly in his book, *Future Shock*. But here, too, by putting Christ at the center of our lives, as the deepest Source of our happiness and stability, we become less dependent on the preservation of things as they are, and less vulnerable to the shocks of change. The Christian has inner resources which others do not have.

But in the true Christian there is an additional strong impulse toward conservatism—one's concern for the preservation of moral and spiritual values. This is much more important than merely preserving the familiar. The Christian believes that in God's revelation in Christ the world has the only pattern of life which will work. The truths of the gospel are unchangeable. The values of the gospel for human happiness and normalcy are unimprovable. Therefore the Christian is suspicious of any change which tampers with these values.

This is the reason the Church has always been conservative, perhaps not always wisely so in specific application, but with a sound instinct. The Church has sensed that there can be no progress beyond the norms found in Christ. The indwelling presence of the Holy Spirit intensifies this kind of conservatism—which may explain its streak of puritanism. And it vigorously rejects that idolatry which worships change for its own sake. It is fearful of any form of humanism which would build its own cultural and ethical Tower of Babel in a vain attempt to be independent of God. It is also suspicious of autonomous creativity, including art in any of its branches, which claims to be a law unto itself.

The Holy Spirit within enables one to bring creativity into the service of Christian conservatism. In this way the values of the gospel will be preserved and propagated at the same time, in ever new and fresh ways. Conservatism without creativity becomes fossilism; creativity without conservatism becomes a booby trap which destroys itself and its environment. Both can be sanctified to the service of God.

PERFECTIONISM VERSUS PERSPECTIVE

Again, we must resolve the tension between *perfectionism* and *perspective*. A canon of culture is perfection. That is, true culture imposes a demand for the best possible workmanship. It distinguishes between good quality and poor quality, whether it is in a suit of clothes or in a special song in church. A thoroughly Christianized seamstress will aim at perfection, for the glory of God, and will never be *content* with shabby work. The same is true for a Christian mechanic, a Christian scholar, or a Christian musician. But trouble arises—and it can be very serious trouble—when perfection becomes our god instead of our reasonable goal. This is perfection*ism*, a cruel, whiplashing tyrant indeed. The only antidote to this perversion is the maintenance of that perspective which keeps things sorted out in the order of their priorities, and which refuses to "lose sight of the forest for the trees." When the most important things are done, some things of lesser importance may have to settle for a little lower level of performance.

Take for instance the question of church music. Choirs and soloists and musicians should perform as well as they can, and constantly strive to improve. But sometimes they must get up and perform anyway, with or without perfection, remembering that, as important as perfection is, spirit and motive are more important—and above all, the anointing of the Holy Spirit. Some of our smaller churches need to spruce up, but some of our larger churches are in danger of supposing they must put on a weekly professional concert. As a consequence what is intended to be worship becomes a religious show.

When culture becomes an end in itself, it ceases to be Christian; it is then a liability in the house of God instead of an asset. Very timely is the warning of J. B. Phillips: "It is natural and right that the worship we offer to God in public should be one of the highest possible quality. But that must not lead us to conceive a musically 'Third-program' as to a god who prefers the professional rendering of a cynical professional choir to the ragged bawling of sincere but untutored hearts."[2]

In the home, also, this tension between perfection and perspective needs urgently to be resolved. Atmosphere is more important than spotlessness. The liveliness of children and youth who at least are *at home* is more important than the immaculate drapes and quiet hush of an exhibition house. A recent cartoon showed a mother standing in the doorway with a guest, viewing and hearing the bedlam of the living room, with one child practicing the piano, two others on the other side of the room practicing wind instruments, all with strained, screwed-up faces, and sheets of music littering the floor. The mother's apologetic comment was, "Our home just reeks with culture." Well, if they are going to become cultured, some temporary non-culture may have to be accepted as the price.

72

The lesson one Christian worker learned along this line was reported in the *Herald of Holiness* some years ago. When entertaining in her home after service one night, she caught the eye of a guest noticing some dust on the furniture. When the time was ripe, she explained quietly: "You know, total obedience means different things to different people. With me it means keeping my house on the altar. You see, I am Swedish, and I was born with a hatred of dirt in my blood. So when I was married, even though in the Lord's work, I felt it my duty to put my house first. When calls came to help I always went, but only after I was satisfied that I could leave an immaculate house. One day such a call came early in the morning to pray with a dying woman who was not sure of her readiness to meet the Lord. As usual I went about my own work, only to find when in the afternoon I reached the woman's side that she had lapsed into unconsciousness. She died soon without knowing that I had come. I went home to weep bitterly through much of the night. I promised God that never again would I put my home ahead of a need. Now, when calls come I drop everything and go. My house is not always as nice as I would wish it to be, but I feel that I now have a more Christian scale of values."

It would be better to allow the Spirit to resolve the tension between perfection and perspective without having to suffer such traumatic discipline. But at least the resolution of the two is implicit in the Spirit-filled life, where the basic desire is to do one's best for God, yet not allow some fancied "best" to become a god.

OWNERSHIP VERSUS STEWARDSHIP

Finally, there is the tension between *possession* and *consecration*, *ownership* and *stewardship*, *relative affluence* and *sacrifice*, *attachment* and *detachment*. We consecrate our all to God, yet fill our homes with beautiful artifacts. We rejoice in our stewardship and also rejoice in our possessions. We pray for the extension of the gospel, yet live in comfort. Do these apparent contradictions brand us as self-deluded pretenders? Must all our attempts to reconcile them in the end be labelled as mere sophistries? Or is there a true synthesis found in holiness itself?

On the one hand, the holy life impels toward culture, and culture implies the appreciation for and enjoyment of all things beautiful. Furthermore, this level of living fosters normalcy; that is, Christians should be models in the world, exhibiting what normal, everyday living should be like. It should be happy, healthy living, focused in the church, the family, and the community—three social units which require property and accessories. The Christian home should be the most attractive spot in the block—not in showcase veneer, but in orderliness, harmony, and efficiency. This does not require a lot of things, but it requires some. If there is to be reading, there must be books. If there is to be music, there must be instruments. If there is to be conversation, there must be chairs to sit on. If there is to be health, there must be facilities for the care and comfort of the body.

Since this earth is a material place, those who live in it must use materials—physical, spatial, formful, representing material values measurable in monetary terms. Christianity endorses this. In a sense, biblical religion (as William Temple once reminded us) is the most materialistic religion in the world. It does not treat material possessions and artistic skills in the manufacture of artifacts as evils, but as necessary for normal living, as aids in personal development, and as means for serving God.[3] But the punch line is that these accessories may as well be cultural even while they are functional. If chairs are legitimate at all, isn't it just as legitimate for them to be beautiful instead of ugly? Therefore some measure of possession, sufficient for mental health and vocational efficiency and cultural enrichment, is not only tolerated by Christianity but belongs inherently to it. When we consider that a church building was not constructed for almost 200 years after the death of Christ, we can be thankful that many Christians had homes suitable for the housing of churches.

We have had enough of writers and preachers throwing at Christian youth the example of some wild-eyed Communist, as if this were a model to emulate, and as if the Communist put the Christian to shame. What is too often almost eulogized is not healthy dedication but feverish fanaticism. These people have surrendered their humanity to become soulless cogs in a tyrannical machine. This is dedication without love, without kindness, and without compassion. This is no example to be held up to young Christians as a means of embarrassing them and goading them. Christians are to live as redeemed men, not as revolutionaries. We are saved men, not saviors. We rejoice in what Christ has done: we don't boast in what we are going to do.

Jesus came to give His life a ransom for many, but He was the most relaxed Man in His crowd. There was nothing hard or tense or cold about Him. He was not devoted to a cause with a capital C; but to God, with a capital G. True, Jesus demands our all; but when He gets our all, He turns us into normal men and women who can laugh and play as well as weep and pray. He doesn't expect us to copy humorless, loveless, heartless tools of a Satanic kingdom of darkness.

Yet this same holiness of life impels toward sacrificial living as a normal expression of our stewardship. The exact balance between legitimate possession and willing dispossession for Jesus' sake is never easy to find. In fact, it must be found, in the last analysis, by each individual in the light of God's specific will for him. At this point, God's sovereignty is the harmonizing principle. Stewardship does not mean a flat uniformity in the way we serve God. It does not even mean equity. There will forever be inequity in this imperfect world between, for example, the sacrifice of the missionary and Mr. Average Christian, between a Wesley who declared a life-commitment to poverty and the more affluent Methodists in whose comfortable homes he was entertained.

Perfect equity will have to await the adjustment of eternity. But in the meanwhile we can individually be at peace by accepting gladly the sovereignty of God for us, exactly in the same way a soldier must accept the authority of the state in time of war. He knows that some back home are living near-normal lives while he is exposed to hardship and death. He knows that deployment of men and resources can never be accomplished on the basis of exact fairness, to say nothing of private preferences. This is the way it is. So likewise the Christian brings himself under God's total sovereignty, and allows God to deploy him as He will. For some this will be service abroad, for others service at home; for some small salaries, for others larger salaries; for some cottages, for others comfortable houses; for some, few cultural supports; for others, many cultural supports.

The rebellious will complain bitterly and loudly. The dedicated man who accepts God's sovereignty, and with it his own deployment, will be happy in spite of the imbalance. He will know that all are equal in Christ, and that God has His own secret ways of bestowing more honor upon what Paul calls the "uncomely parts" (I Cor. 12:23). In the meanwhile he will be inwardly cultured and outwardly enjoy the fruits of culture as much as circumstances will allow. At the same time, his brother at home who supports him by his generous offerings will consider himself equally the Lord's and equally at the Lord's disposal for sacrifice or service. Equally, too, will he find his supreme joy, not in things, but in Christ. He too is mindful that he must "use this world, as not abusing it: for the fashion of this world passeth away" (I Cor. 7:31).

Therefore the happy, disinterested consecration of the true Christian is the best spiritual state for learning how to balance austerity and expenditure in one's personal life. "Brother Andrew" (in *God's Smuggler*) illustrates this truth. So devoted were he and Corrie to the work that in their self-forgetfulness they came close to jeopardizing mental and physical health. Even their clothes came out of the refugee bins, to save money. But his eyes were opened by a scathing letter from a donor, which closed: "God will send you what your family needs and what your work needs too. You are a mature Christian, Brother Andrew. Act like one." This letter was followed by Corrie's acute embarrassment when they were invited to a social function and she discovered that she had nothing suitable to wear. Brother Andrew commented: "And suddenly I saw that this was part of a whole pattern of poverty into which we had fallen, a dark, brooding, pinched attitude that hardly went with the Christ of the open heart that we were preaching to others." While they continued to live frugally, they stopped living like ragged orphans, as if it were some kind of virtue. He says, "We are learning to take joy in the physical things that God provides. Corrie bought some dresses. We went ahead with the tearing down of a wall so that she could walk directly from the house to her kitchen."[4]

6

The Stewardship of the Fine Arts

Paul Tillich defined religion as ultimate concern. For the Christian this ultimate concern is the glory of God. As far as man is concerned, God's glory is manifest in redemption. This was the governing principle of Christ and the Cross. Since that is true, it must equally be the governing principle of discipleship. Taking up the cross means adopting this redemption motif as the rule of life. Holiness (in turn) means that what we have chosen has been worked into the very marrow of our being, and is being allowed to work its way out in our total value system and lifestyle.

> *My friend, we never choose the better part,*
> *Until we set the cross up in the heart.*
> *I know I cannot live until I die,*
> *Till I am nailed upon it wild and high,*

And sleep in the tomb for a full three days dead,
With angels at the feet and at the head.
But then, in a great brightness shall I arise,
To walk with stiller feet below the skies.
                    —EDWIN MARKHAM
                         (Surrexi)

ALL OR NOTHING

This leads us straight to the concept of stewardship. In repentance we acknowledge God's ownership. In consecration we reconfirm that acknowledgment and face up to its explicit, thorough, all-embracing demands. The steward identifies himself totally with the business of his Master. He is not in business for himself, not even covertly on the side, in what he thinks is his spare time. The interests of his Master have become his, solely and exclusively. For the Christian the Master is Christ and his business is the kingdom of God.

This will settle the question of the comparative claims of the secular and the sacred. A young woman explaining her marital difficulties said, "When my husband and I were married we were pronounced one, but we have been quarreling ever since trying to decide which is the one." Something like this is happening in the debate over the secular and the sacred. The modern trend in theology is to pronounce them one. The question is, Which is the one? The Christian principle of stewardship confirms the oneness, but resolves the tension by declaring that the sacred is *the* one. Stewardship is the recognition of God's total ownership, hence the sanctity of the whole. This does *not* mean that the whole is automatically holy; it means that the authority of the sacred extends to the whole. The whole must be sanctified—*purged* of that which is not "sanctifiable" and the rest dedicated to the service of God.

The consecration of every part of life to the control and service of God is so essentially obligatory in the divine-human scheme of things that to fail to consecrate is to desecrate. Marcus Dods reminds us,

> He is not the only prodigal who in riotous pleasure or vain display brings himself to beggary; but he is the prodigal who in any way wastes the powers and means God gave him to effect substantial good. . . . It seems a matter of no importance . . . that we are living for ourselves; we think that living for God is a height of consecration that some may aspire to, but that it is no law of life for all; but we come to find that it is just this which makes the difference, and that all we have done on any other footing had far better have been left undone. . . . If we have spent our portion, our talents, our opportunities, our life, in striving to please ourselves . . . then manifestly we have as thoroughly alienated ourselves and our portion from God as if we had spent it on riotous living.[1]

The whole of life must be laid at Christ's feet. The whole of life must be redemptive. The whole of life must forward the kingdom of God. The whole of life must be devoted to glorifying God and seeking the souls of men in one way or another. This is involved not alone in being a specialist, such as a preacher or missionary, but in simply being a Christian. As Francis Schaeffer expresses it, "The Bible says God made the whole man, the whole man is to know salvation, and the whole man is to know the Lordship of Christ."[2]

Then the fine arts too must be brought under the rod of stewardship. We must not only pray to the glory of God, but sing too. And when we sing "Crown Him Lord of All" we are not authorized to add under our breath, "except the fine arts."

There can be no independent compartments in the Christian life. There can be no pockets of interest or activity which either are a law unto themselves or are ruled by pagan laws. The Christian says good-bye to autonomy forever. We cannot serve God with our hearts and at the same time serve the world, the flesh, and the devil with the fine arts. We cannot live under one set of motives, goals, and standards when we pray, then come under a completely different and alien pattern of motives, goals, and standards when we take up our brush, baton, or pen (or when we play records!). This is why the famous and internationally loved Mahalia Jackson died relatively poor. Though she had many fabulous offers, she refused to sing in any place where liquor was sold. She took the lordship of Christ seriously.

This basic principle, which cannot be violated without revealing an elemental falseness to Christ, will structure—in some cases restructure—our philosophy of art. What is the purpose of art? What is the meaning of beauty? That painting hanging on the wall—what are its credentials? What principles give it its right to hang there? The Christian must answer in the light of the Cross and in the light of stewardship. If our personal relationship to Christ is real, there is a glad willingness so to answer. The debate is over.

Any form of idolatry is therefore ruled out. This includes the idolatry of making the fine arts central in one's life. Some people live for music, others for painting, others for hobbies. These pursuits become ends in themselves. Nothing has any right to be an end in itself. God is the Christian's end, and all else a means to the end of glorifying God. What cannot serve this end will be resolutely jettisoned.

The technical canons for the evaluation of a specific form or work of art are not now under consideration. We are thinking of Christian canons. When we bring these to bear we must ask, first, What is the aim? The most dangerous and vicious art is that which is good art technically but devoted to the wrong ends. Second, What are its effects? Is what it does to the viewer or listener or reader strengthening or weakening, ennobling or debasing?

That people are either coarsened or refined by their literature and art is incontestable. Someone has said, "Show me the songs that a nation sings and I will forecast the moral future of that nation." We cannot separate the aesthetics of

81

a people from their ethics. Low ethics will prostitute the arts, and decadent forms of art will feed low ethics. This is true even if technical excellence is improved. Pornography is pornography no matter how skillfully and artistically lithographed. Rot is rot even though bound in hard cover and assigned as required reading for high school and college students.

A faithful steward who is seeking to sanctify the fine arts is bound to insist that the arts he enjoys and the arts he patronizes pass these Christian tests. But he will also seek to involve the arts as *tools* in his total stewardship.

THE ARTS AS TOOLS

First, this will include the legitimate use of art for *personal enrichment*. God can use the arts to fashion one into a better person, and thus a more useful person. This may be brought about either through the enjoyment of sharing the beauty created by others or through the satisfaction of creating one's own. For both appreciation and achievement make disciplinary demands. There must be the discipline of concentration, of discrimination, of emotional involvement. And if we ourselves are seeking mastery, the discipline of patience and persistence and, yes, the discipline of perception are also involved.

Art (in any of its various forms) may refresh our spirits, and thus send us back to our Christian work toned up. Art may sharpen our discernment of what is proper and right. Art should always be a prompting toward the worship of God. It can often open our souls to new heights of communion with God. In these various ways we become richer persons and better able to glorify Him. A Christian who has a cultivated taste for fine foods but none for fine music is a Christian whose level of life is too low. His capacity for God is infantile and undeveloped, to say the least.

Second, sanctified parents will endeavor to utilize art

as a means of *molding their children*. Everything in one's home is a part of the total culture and has a bearing on the total input into a child's character. This includes the pictures on the wall, the books on the shelves, the magazines on the table, the music that is listened to, and also the conversation —including the things that are laughed at and the jokes that are told. If there is coarseness in the home, the children will be coarse and will not learn to discern between the proper and improper, the cheap and vulgar, or the refined and noble. They will grow up with a flippant attitude toward sex and the human body because they have imbibed it from crudeness in the home. They will have no sense of wonder, no quick sensitivity to beauty, and thus will be irreverent toward the church and sacred things. Those who are insensitive to the sacred are generally also the ones who are insensitive to the beautiful sunset and the blue of a summer sky. For coarseness and insensitivity are all of a piece.

We have not fully appreciated this potential cultural transference. A youngster who learns accurate pitch so that he can tell whether or not a tone is true will better understand the meaning of honesty—whether or not the spoken word is true. As he listens to music he can say, That does not ring true; when he listens to a sermon, he can also say, That does not ring true. This kind of transference may not be automatic, certainly not perfect. What is suggested here is only that the training of the mind through aesthetics may condition a child to a more intelligent and ready grasp of ethical principles, and the niceties of ethical distinctions.[3]

But at least cultivated tastes in music, art, and literature may give a child distaste for the trash of the world, and this one advantage is a big push toward the voluntary acceptance of total Christian standards.

Not long ago an evangelist was visiting in the home of a concerned father of two small girls. The father was expressing his fear to stay in the little church in the community; for, he said, "In 25 years that church has not held a single one of its youth." They had "gone to the dogs" and to the devil. As the evangelist talked to him, he became aware of something other than the father's simple earnestness. Culturally, the home was vacant. There was not a picture, musical instrument, or book to be seen. Probably some comic books could have been uncovered. The girls amused themselves on their own (TV hadn't reached them yet). The evangelist's imagination projected itself into the future. When teen years came with bursting desires and energies, and boys with flashy cars beckoned with their excitement, and the gang sought entertainment elsewhere, would this culturally empty home be too dull to hold them? If so, the church would, of course, be blamed.

As the evangelist reflected, he surmised that this home was typical of that little church which had tragically lost its young people. Surely we must not conclude that a piano in the home will guarantee the salvation of our children. But if properly used and combined with a whole arsenal of interesting activities, plus training in the relevant aesthetic standards, such things may play a very significant part. A minister, in pinpointing some possible reasons why seven brothers were all in the church and five in the ministry, said that his father made it a point to have plenty of new, bright, worthwhile books lying around all during their growing years.

This kind of culture is no substitute for regenerating and sanctifying grace, but it can be a powerful ally. By its aid the divine grace is more apt to reach its fruition in stable, mature character.

Third, the sanctified Christian will desire to utilize the fine arts as *a means of evangelism.* Very careful thinking is needed here lest we settle for some cheap and inappropriate means of immediate gains and pay the price of lasting and irreparable loss.

Just as the home has a duty to inculcate that kind of culture which is most compatible with the Christian life, and which elevates the taste toward the highest and best, so does the church have a similar obligation. The church fails in this phase of its ministry if it treats all music media as being on an equal level, and makes no distinctions between a medium which is appropriate for the sanctuary and that which is most appropriate for the dance floor. If the church makes no distinction, how can we expect our untrained converts to perceive any difference?

In a paper entitled "How Does Your Church Music Rate?" Audrey Darling[4] asks two leading questions: "Is the music appropriate?" and, "Is it fulfilling its mission—that of a ministry?" She goes on to insist that Christ made no place in His ministry for sentimentality (cf. Luke 9:59-62). She comments: "A song with over-familiar words dethrones God to a human level. Respect, reverence, and glory are denied Him." She identifies two examples: "I'm going to talk to the Man Upstairs" and "I want to be a friend of Christ, mmm—and a little bit more." May I support Miss Darling by adding, This is a cheap desecration of that which is holy. It is juvenile gush which lacks awareness of who God is. With some thoughtless persons it may be more immature than vicious. This is why the church has a teaching responsibility in these areas.

We are living in a day of blurred lines and nondescript grays. In the popular mind almost nothing is wrong, and almost anything can find its defenders, from pornography to homosexuality, from nudity to "rock" in the house of God. We are shocked by the far-out immorality outside of the church, but let us not forget that much of that is the result of a gradual erosion of ideals and standards inside of the Church. If we do not want the fruit, we had better not feed the root. And we cannot separate ethical ideals and standards from the forms of worship and evangelism which utilize the fine arts. We cannot foster an erotic type of music and expect to succeed in avoiding the erosion of standards and ideals in the area of ethics.

We must carefully distinguish between that which is anointed and that which is merely animated; that which is spiritual and that which is merely spirited; that which is truly inspiring and that which is merely amusing; that which really blesses and that which merely tickles; that which directs the attention to God and that which is pure entertainment with the attention terminally on the performance and the performer.

The artistic medium can defeat its purpose. In religion, whether in worship or in evangelism, the purpose is to create an atmosphere of true repentance, reverence, and God-consciousness. If the medium is presented with a degree of perfection that inspires admiration rather than reverence, and leaves people saying, "What a beautiful voice!" or, "What skillful playing!"—then the very excellence of the art has been an impediment in the fulfillment of its function. Moreover if in seeking to convey a message through music or art an excessive amount of drama and theatrics is incorporated, the audience will be fascinated by watching, but will not be convicted by listening to the Holy Spirit. They may be emotionally moved, even to an altar, and experience the catharsis of an emotional experience—all without true repentance or Spirit-regeneration. And the undiscerning Christian won't know the difference.

That which is most powerful in moving emotions of people either toward the physical or toward God is the artistic medium, not the words which are supposed to contain the message. We cannot change the basic effect of certain kinds of rhythm and beat, simply by attaching to them a few religious or semi-religious words. The beat will still get through, to the blood of the participants and the listeners. Words are timid things. Decibels and beat are bold things, which can easily bury the words under an avalanche of sound. The bit of religion tagged on will only lend to the whole performance a fake aura of sanctity, but will not be an instrument which the Holy Spirit can use to bring awakening and conviction.

The famous radio personality Art Linkletter is quoted as claiming that pop music has contributed greatly to the susceptibility of modern youth to drugs. A Kansas City psychiatrist says: "Rock by its very nature destroys the inhibitions." It thus conditions the person to the bizarre, the irregular, and the uncontrolled, making him an easy mark for other forms of impulsive experimentation, this doctor claims. If this observation made by a professional entertainer and confirmed by many psychiatrists is valid, the Church ought to listen, and ought not to be so foolish as to use forms which loosen personality moorings, instead of reinforcing them. This is the day of the big sound, hypnotic and overpowering—a mighty good tool for the devil but a poor one for the Church.

The fact that some people may like this or that is not sufficient reason for the Church to use it. The Church should lead the way in such standards, not abjectly follow every fad and custom which happens to be "in" at the moment. The Church has no business adopting the philosophy, "If you can't lick 'em, join 'em." We should be governed by basic and eternal Christian principles. There are music forms, whether secular or sacred, which create moods of pensiveness, of idealism, of awareness of beauty, of aspiration, and of holy joyousness. There are other forms of music which create moods of recklessness and sensual excitement. Surely it doesn't take much judgment to know which forms are most appropriate for religious functions.

In the long run, those forms which are most compatible to the function of worship will also be the most effective in evangelism. All one needs to do is to think of the powerful effect of the simple singing of Ira Sankey, Homer Rodeheaver, and more recently, Bev Shea, Gary Moore, and the Bill Gaithers, to realize that this is the way to reach the heart of the masses for God—the clothing of a *real message* in an appealing and moving melody that *fits the message*, and then the singing of the words in the manner which transmits *verbal clarity*. "I don't want the music to kill the words," explained a wise and experienced saint.

Perhaps we would do well to listen to David Wilkerson, who says:

> Christian rock groups are brought to our youth crusades by sponsoring churches. They appear on my stage with their drums and loud guitars, handclapping their way through songs that speak of Jesus, but with the primitive beat borrowed from the Beatles or some other hard rock group. I try not to act surprised, offended, or ashamed. You see, I want so much to relate to these young people.

> The kids in the audience seem to love every beat. They clap, they smile, they relate, they turn on, and they get excited. But something inside me, deep in my soul, does not feel right. There's a small hurt which I can't suppress; I feel uneasy. Somehow I am grieved, and I can't explain it. I feel as though the Holy Spirit within me does not witness to the rock sounds in the middle of a salvation meeting. I also have a sense, an inner knowledge, that the gentle Holy Spirit is not comfortable in the atmosphere this music creates.[5]

Others, such as Bob Larson, Jack Wyrtzen, and Jack Hyles, are just as positive if not more so in their disapproval. These are not reactionary old men, nor are they armchair theorists; they are "with it" men who are working constantly and successfully with youth.

This does not put the Church in a straitjacket of narrow traditional forms. There are many bright new sounds abroad which glorify God. Various styles—country, folk, gospel, as well as hymns and anthems—have relative degrees of value and suitability. Guitars have their place as well as organs. Amateurs should not be shamed into silence. Lively rhythm may at times not only be permissible but appropriate. And as David Wilkerson says, even loudness is all right, provided it is not mixed with lewdness. But every form should be compelled to pass four tests:

1. *Suitability*—to the particular place and occasion.

2. *Appropriateness*—to the subject matter, which is Christ. Is He cheapened? Is He reduced to mere human stature? Is there reverence or levity? (or worse yet, *blasphemy?*)

3. *Communication*—getting through with a biblically clear message. It can fail here in two ways: the words may be goo and gush—unsound religious nonsense; or *good words* may be blocked out either by poor diction, incompatible music form, or untempered decibels.

4. *Spirituality*—a conductor of spiritual effects, not sensual and physical. Does it reach the heart or the heels? Does it quicken the conscience and woo to God or dull the deep, spiritual senses? Even so-called "soul" music is not necessarily *spiritual*.

The difference in good or bad church music is the emotion generated. On the one hand there is that which is selfward and manward; on the other that which is Godward, upward, and *decisive*. This is why in all the various possible forms, sooner or later a line is reached beyond which the music ceases to be a good conductor of spiritual edification, and instead becomes a conductor of fleshly stimulation.

This is the basic indictment against jazz and "rock." "In some strange, psychological manner the pronounced beat . . . touches a responsive chord in the lower nature of man," writes William L. Banks.[6] The attempt therefore to wed the loud rock sounds and beat to words of love and devotion is self-destructive, for it violates what Calvin Seerveld insists is the *sine qua non* of art, the "law of coherence."[7] The symbolical meaning of the "rock" sounds is contradictory to the symbolical meaning of the religious text. In the words of Harold B. Kuhn, "A serious or quasi-serious theme is typically paralleled by a form of over-music whose mood is incongruous with it."[8] To combine some things is to tear down walls which should not be torn down. The result is irreparable damage to those who uncritically absorb it.

And the contradictoriness is more than merely a matter of cultural conditioning (though at many less serious points this admittedly plays a large part). The nature of the primitive beat is such that the incompatibility is inherent.

Jack Paar's experience in Africa should say something to us. On a TV interview he reported that on a recent African safari he and his group had with them some musicians who performed before a group of particularly primitive and untouched natives. As long as the musicians played conventional music structured by melody, form, and harmony, there was no reaction. But when they shifted to rock, immediately the natives came alive—this was their beat! Yet this is the form of music—this which appeals "to the primitive and the primeval in man" (Kuhn)—which we imagine we can baptize into the service of the gentle, wooing Holy Spirit! To associate Christ with its dissipating, hypnotic power may produce excitement but not spiritual depth or maturity.

Some readers will point to the conversions which apparently occur following the use of religious rock, with the dubious assumption that even one soul saved is a divine endorsement. The question is, What is true, appropriate, and inherently sound? In some of our sincere but misguided evangelism, the Spirit reaches around our gimmicks and finds some conductor over which spiritual energy can flow to reach a hungry heart. If the Word is preached, if sincere testimonies are given, if there is an atmosphere of warm love, of course there will be fruit. But let us not naively suppose the deafening rock music has been the instrument. But was it not the promise of such music that brought the kids in? Perhaps in some cases, yes. But teens are always attracted by groups of spicy, lively teens. What proof is there that the same kids could not have been brought in by a smashing musicale supported by exciting but more compatible music?

Bob Larson publishes a convincing letter from a young Christian radio announcer who, as a disc jockey, believed that he could use this kind of music to spread the gospel. He writes:

> I knew that rock had strong influential powers and I reasoned that maybe it could be used to spread the Gospel and I stood firm in those feelings. What I wouldn't admit was that I couldn't worship the Lord while I was hearing those drums and other instruments pound out the rhythm. I felt the driving sound and rhythm in my body and mind. It was a flesh trip. . . . I believe in making a joyful noise unto the Lord but when the music leaves the spiritual realm and becomes a driving force it goes into the physical realm.[9]

When this young man became really honest with himself and with God, he saw that he was only rationalizing, and as a result arresting his own spiritual development without benefiting anyone else. So he surrendered his myth.

Fortunately there are signs that the religious rock fad has passed its crest and that, at least among evangelicals, some who were at first tolerant are taking a sober second look.

In our use of the fine arts as tools, let us think through the philosophy which should govern us as Bible-believing Christians. We want to build with "gold, silver, precious stones," rather than with "wood, hay, stubble," which in the end will be burned (I Cor. 3:12-13).

Reference Notes

PREFACE:

1. H. Richard Niebuhr, *Christ and Culture* (New York: Harper and Bros., 1951), p. 33.

2. *Ibid.*

CHAPTER 1:

1. Harry Blamires, *The Christian Mind* (London: S.P.C.K., 1966), p. 80.

2. Fred P. Thompson, Jr., "Man's Need to Learn," *Christianity Today*, May 26, 1972, p. 4.

3. Quoted in the *National Inquirer*, Nov., 1972.

4. *Art Education*, June, 1971.

5. "The Responsibility of the Church in Our Age," originally printed in Vol. 165 of *The Annals of the American Academy of Political and Social Science*, Philadelphia, Jan., 1933. Quoted in *Christian News*, Jan. 15, 1968.

6. Francis Schaeffer, *Death in the City* (London: Inter-Varsity Press, 1969), p. 75.

7. Thompson, *op. cit.*

8. H. R. Rookmaaker, *Modern Art and the Death of a Culture* (London: Inter-Varsity Press, 1970), p. 36.

9. *Ibid.*, p. 38.

CHAPTER 2:

1. *Herald of Holiness*, March 1, 1972.

2. *U.S. News and World Report*, Mar. 20, 1972, reports a very recent upsurge in interest in classical music. We can be thankful for this "cloud" the size of "a man's hand." But it remains to be seen how strong and penetrative it will be in elevating general tastes.

3. Quoted by Dr. David Ward-Steinman in reviewing four books by Schafer, a Canadian composer and teacher. Review published in *Newsletter*, fall, 1971, Contemporary Music Project, a project of Music Educators National Conference, Washington, D.C.

4. Quoted by George Oppenheimer in *Newsday*. Original statement made on "NBC Comment," moderated by Edwin Newman.

5. Schaeffer, *op. cit.*, p. 46.

6. *Ibid.*, p. 12.

7. Blamires, *op. cit.*, p. 112.

8. Clyde S. Kilby, *Christianity and Aesthetics* (Chicago: Inter-Varsity Press, 1961), p. 22.

9. *Ibid.*

10. *Ibid.*, p. 23.

11. Addison H. Leitch, "View of Man Sets Education Tone," *Universitas*, Nov., 1972.

CHAPTER 3:

1. C. S. Lewis, *Miracles* (New York: The Macmillan Co., 1963), p. 163.

CHAPTER 4:

1. R. O. Hurst, ed., *Pharmacy Apprenticeship Studies* (Toronto, Ont.: The University of Toronto Press, 1934-37), p. 155. This example, so surprising in such a source, was used to illustrate the importance of literary breadth and competence, whether in pharmacy, the ministry, or any other vocation.

2. Eula May Miller, *I Am a Woman* (Chicago: Moody Press, 1967), p. 58.

3. *Reader's Digest*, Nov., 1968.

4. Oswald Chambers, *My Utmost for His Highest* (New York: Dodd, Mead and Co., 1935), p. 213.

CHAPTER 5:

1. Blamires, *op. cit.*, p. 130.

2. J. B. Phillips, *Your God Is Too Small* (New York: The Macmillan Co., n.d.), p. 44.

3. Extreme poverty is not necessarily a means of grace. It does not, per se, assure either superior culture or character. Extreme poverty, squalor, dissipation, and disorderliness are often found together.

4. Brother Andrew, *God's Smuggler* (Kansas City: Nazarene Publishing House, 1971), pp. 168 f.

CHAPTER 6:

1. Marcus Dods, *Parables of Our Lord* (Old Tappan, N.J.: Fleming H. Revell Co., n.d.), p. 350.

2. Schaeffer, *op. cit.*, p. 75.

3. Cf. W. T. Purkiser, *et al.*, *Exploring Our Christian Faith* (Kansas City: Beacon Hill Press, 1960), p. 475.

4. Member of the music faculty of Canadian Nazarene College, Winnipeg, Manitoba.

5. David Wilkerson, *Get Your Hands off My Throat* (Grand Rapids, Mich.: Zondervan Publishing House, 1971), pp. 51-52.

6. William L. Banks, *The Black Church in the United States* (Chicago: Moody Press, 1972), p. 114.

7. Calvin Seerveld, *A Christian Critique of Art* (Toronto, Canada: Association for Reformed Scientific Studies, 1963), pp. 44-45.

8. Harold B. Kuhn, "The Multi-Medium Man," *Christianity Today*, May 24, 1968.

9. Bob Larson, *Rock & the Church* (Carol Stream, Ill.: Creation House, 1971), p. 61.

For Further Reading

Blamires, Harry. *The Christian Mind*. London: S.P.C.K., 1966.

Fogarty, Richard J. *Rock—the Quiet Revolution*. Schroon Lake, N.Y.: Word of Life Fellowship, Inc., 1972.

Kilby, Clyde S. *Christianity and Aesthetics*. Chicago: Inter-Varsity Press, 1961.

Larson, Bob. *Rock and the Church*. Denver, Colo.: Bob Larson Ministries, 1971.

Lewis, C. S. *The Abolition of Man*. New York: The Macmillan Company, 1947.

Mollenkott, Virginia R. *Adamant and Stone Chips*. Waco, Tex.: Word Books, 1967.

Niebuhr, H. Richard. *Christ and Culture*. New York: Harper and Brothers, 1951.

Purkiser, W. T., editor. *Exploring Our Christian Faith*. Kansas City, Mo.: Beacon Hill Press, 1960. Chapter XXIII.

Rookmaaker, H. R. *Modern Art and the Death of a Culture*. London: Inter-Varsity Press, 1970.

Schaeffer, Francis A. *Escape from Reason*. London: Inter-Varsity Fellowship, 1968.

———. *The God Who Is There*. London: Hodder and Stoughton, 1969.

Seerveld, Calvin. *A Christian Critique of Art*. Ontario, Canada: The Association of Reformed Scientific Studies. Christian Perspective Series, 1963.

Wellman, Wendell. *Right Dress!* Kansas City, Mo.: Beacon Hill Press of Kansas City, 1967.

Wilkerson, David. *Get Your Hands off My Throat*. Grand Rapids, Mich.: Zondervan Publishing House, 1971.